To: Lisa & Andy

Cunee

Chef Table Experience

2022

FIND THE BEST AND FRESHEST INGREDIENTS YOU POSSIBLY CAN

· THEN PREPARE THEM SIMPLY.

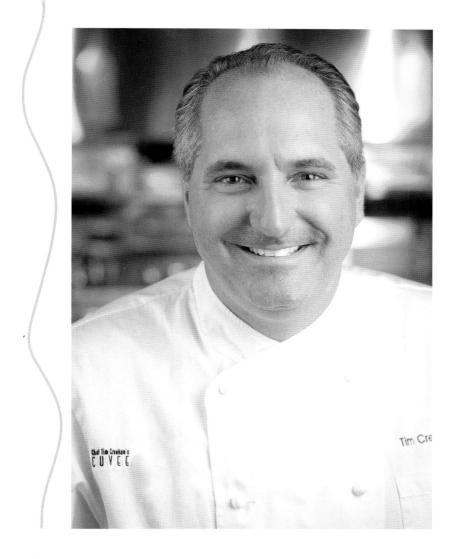

SIMPLE CUISINE

TIM CREEHAN

Gulf Coast Favorites from
Chef Creehan's restaurants,
classes & special events.

Chef Tim Creehan and Company, Inc.
755 Grand Blvd., Suites B105-332
Miramar Beach, FL 32550
timcreehan.com

TIM CREEHAN

FOOD & OTHER PHOTOGRAPHY

Photography Copyright © 2004—Chef Tim Creehan and Company, Inc.
Sailing Photos—Michael Belk, Michael Belk and Company
    Photos of the Schooner Daniel Webster Clements were shot in
    Destin, Florida. AJ's Daniel Webster Clements Sailing Cruise is
    home to the beautiful wooden schooner, Daniel Webster Clements.
Scott Brouwer—Food Photographer
Karim Shamsi-Basha—Food Photographer
Dill Beaty—Food Photographer
Thai Chicken Salad Photo—*Cooking Light*® magazine
Other Copyrighted Photographs © 2004
Andrew Eccles—Amy Grant and Vince Gill Photo
Harrison McClary—Tammy Cochran Photo
Theresa Johnson—Steve and Angel Cropper Photo
Denise M. Creehan—Steve Cropper Photo
Denise M. Creehan—Amy Grant and Chef Creehan Photo

COVER PHOTOGRAPHY

Stephen Ramsey

Print ISBN: 978-0-9634545-2-2
e-book ISBN: 978-0-87197-567-6

Library of Congress Number: 2003111371
Manufactured by

 Favorite Recipes® Press

Favorite Recipes® Press is an imprint of Southwestern Publishing
Group, Inc., 2451 Atrium Way, Nashville, Tennessee 37214.
Southwestern Publishing Group is a wholly owned subsidiary
of Southwestern/Great American, Inc., Nashville, Tennessee.

Designed by Designs by Denise, Inc.—Santa Rosa Beach, FL

Printed in China
10 9 8 7 6 5 4 3 2

PHILOSOPHY

When I was still in my teens, I learned two very important life lessons: number one, if you don't absolutely love what you do, you're probably on the wrong path. And number two, once you find the right path, always give more than is expected of you.

I have learned that life is about growing, about learning and meeting challenges—and occasionally even surpassing them. That's why I'm constantly challenging myself to look for ways to create new and delicious dishes that are both simple and easy to prepare. Cooking is an art form; it involves feeling. Recipes have no emotion. By making the recipes in this book uniquely your own, you provide the heart—you provide the soul. I hope this inspires you to use your own imagination and creativity to share the joy of cooking with those you love.

If you cook "from the heart," you want only the best for those at your table. May I offer two secrets to my success?

Find the best and freshest ingredients you possibly can—then prepare them simply.

CHEF TIM CREEHAN

DEDICATION

This book is dedicated to my wonderful parents, John and Marybeth Creehan. My mother is a fabulous cook! She has a gift for making people feel welcome and comfortable. And when it comes to food, my dad is the world's best audience— he loves to eat! I will always remember my parents' zest for living and how much eating and entertaining has meant to my family. It started generations before—those smells, tastes, and memories that came from the kitchen. My parents handed down recipes and passed along traditions that started with three incredible cooks: my Italian grandmother Genevieve Vignone, my Italian great-grandmother Mary Vignone, and my Irish grandmother Elizabeth "Bumper" Creehan. They brought the best of their native cuisines and traditions to their family tables in this country. To all of them I am so grateful.

SPECIAL THANKS

Denise Creehan, Art Direction

Jeanie Brooke, Editor

Les Lovoy, Copywriter

Robert Hasker, Editorial Assistant

Dennis Stiffler, Ph.D., Beef Expert

Kristen Collett, Assistant Food Stylist

Mark Hendrick, Digital Retouching

Diane Prather, Edgar Allen Crow, Props

Deanna Hemby, Assistant to Amy Grant & Vince Gill

Bill Campbell, Sailing South, Destin Harbor

Jeanne Dailey, Newman-Dailey Resort Properties, Inc., Vacation Rentals, Destin

And most importantly, to my loyal and dedicated staff for their patience and commitment to excellence.

TABLE OF CONTENTS

A FISH FINDS WATER

by Les Lovoy

Many people never find their true calling. But once in a while, you meet someone who was lucky enough to discover what came naturally, someone who then spends his life living his dream. Such is the case with Tim Creehan. Tim found his calling in his early teens and it was so natural that you might say he was "like a fish that found water."

Born in Hartford, Connecticut, Tim and his family eventually moved to Baton Rouge, Louisiana. Tim remembers, "I was only 14 years old and out looking for a job. I found a job bussing tables at Steak & Ale, and I immediately fell in love with the restaurant business. For me, it was the total experience—the food itself, the textures, the tastes, the preparation—everything!"

It wasn't long before young Creehan moved from the dining room to the kitchen. And he's been there ever since. When he knew that he had discovered his life's calling, he visited one of the finest restaurants in the area. When he asked how he could become an accomplished chef, he didn't know that he was speaking to the internationally acclaimed Chef Philippe Parola, Commandeur des Cordon Bleu de France.

Parola immediately took the impressionable and impassioned young man under his wing. "I saw a lot of myself in Tim . . . his drive, his passion for his chosen profession and his total commitment. It was a privilege to teach him what I knew. Both of us chose the craft at a very young age. In Europe, of course, you are trained for a profession for life. Tim was simply a natural. His love for food and his compassion for people have combined to make him the success he is today."

Under Chef Parola's mentoring, Creehan developed his innate talents and abilities and learned all about the culinary arts. He never attended cooking school. At 21, Tim became one of the youngest Certified Executive Chefs in the American Culinary Federation. He had to work very hard; he studied management, nutrition, and sanitation through college correspondence courses. "It was no 'piece of cake'," he recalls, "I had to *earn* that certification. There were very stringent requirements, not the least of which was that you had to manage your own kitchen for a minimum of seven years. During that critical time, I learned the entire workings of a restaurant operation."

In addition to reinforcing the virtues of the practical versus the formal education, Chef Parola taught his apt student an important lesson about motivation. "When you're looking for a job as a chef, never ask how you are going to be paid," he said. "If you work hard and succeed, the prosperity follows. It's not about the money; it's about learning new things and becoming the best chef you can be."

Creehan says, "I believe that more than ever today; I'm always looking for a new challenge and I strive to be the best chef I can be."

Creehan's zest for living and his passion for cooking have taken him far. Quite literally. In addition to serving as Executive Chef in many of the finest restaurants on the Gulf Coast, he was invited to participate in the American Harvest Promotion at the Hong Kong Hilton for a two-week guest chef appearance with another of his mentors, Chef John Folse. His "quest to be the best" has garnered him numerous awards and accolades, including:

• 2017 DiRoNA Award, Distinguished Restaurants of North America • 2016 Wine Spectator Best of Award of Excellence, *Wine Spectator* magazine • 2015 Restaurateur of the Year, Florida Restaurant & Lodging Association • 2015 TripAdvisor® Hall of Fame • 2013 OpenTable Diner's Choice Awards Top 100 Best American Cuisine • 2013 OpenTable Diner's Choice Awards Top 100 Hottest Restaurant Bars • 2012–2016 Best of the Emerald Coast, *Emerald Coast* magazine • 2011–2016 Best in Destin, *Destin Magazine* • 2011–2017 TripAdvisor® Certificate of Excellence • 2011–2016 Finest on the Emerald Coast, Northwest Florida Daily News • 2010 Golden Spoon Award Hall of Fame, *Florida Trend* magazine • 2010–2017 OpenTable Diner's Choice Award • 2010–2017 Golden Spoon Award, *Florida Trend* magazine • 2008 Special Guest Chef, Entertainment Tonight/Getty Images/Gibson Guitar Lodge, Sundance Film Festival • 2008 96th Air Base Wing Honorary Commander, Eglin Air Force Base • 2006 Regional Culinary Hospitality Award in Fine Dining, *Santé Magazine* • 2005 Restaurant of the Year, Northwest Florida Daily News • 2004 Celebrated Chef, National Pork Council • 2004 DiRoNA Award, Distinguished Restaurants of North America • 2003–2007 Top 25 Restaurants in Florida, Golden Spoon Award Winner, *Florida Trend* magazine • 2003–2015 Wine Spectator Award of Excellence, *Wine Spectator* magazine • 2003–2007 Three Diamond Property, AAA/CAA • 2002 One of Florida's Emerging Culinary Talents, *Bon Appétit* magazine • 2002 Top 250 Restaurant, *Florida Trend* magazine • 2001 Top 200 Restaurant, *Florida Trend* magazine • 2000–2008 Best of the Emerald Coast, *Emerald Coast* magazine • 1999 Shining Star Chef, *Cooking Light* magazine • 1997 DiRoNA Award, Distinguished Restaurants of North America• 1992 Emerald Coast Chef's Challenge, Best of Show Award • 1989 Florida Governor's Cup Seafood Challenge, Second Place • 1987 Baton Rouge Culinary Classic, Gold and Silver Medals • 1987 Acadiana Culinary Classic, Gold and Silver Awards in four categories • 1987 Seafood Challenge of Louisiana, Second Place • 1987 Seafood Challenge of Baton Rouge, First Place

Now happily settled in Florida, Tim Creehan owns the award-winning Cuvee 30A located at 30Avenue. Like his mentor before him, he takes great delight in mentoring the next generation of chefs. "I have a kitchen staff of highly motivated and talented young cooks," he says. "I teach them everything I can and I encourage them to have their own chance at a great career as a chef."

Atypically, Chef Creehan's cooks don't just come and go. "Several of my chefs have been with me for nine years or longer," he says with pride. "It's great to be able to help young people, just like Chef Parola helped me."

Tim's commitment to excellence has earned him the respect and admiration of food critics, peers and students. "Executive Chef and owner Tim Creehan, who turns out delicious dishes—like pepper-crusted tuna with sauteed spinach and a soy ginger sauce—is one of Florida's emerging culinary talents," says Robert Tolf, *Florida Trend* magazine, in a story for *Bon Appétit*. Creehan's culinary influence remains irrevocably ensconced throughout Destin's eateries as their menus continue to capitalize on the popularity of his signature dishes.

Creehan has opened several successful venues along the Gulf Coast, leading to the Restaurateur of the Year award from the FRLA, and finding his latest venture, Cuvee 30A, featured on *Emeril's Florida*. Ever seeking a new challenge, in 1997 Creehan created a nonstick instant marinade and got his invention patented. Grill Plus Instant Marinade has since become part of the Kinder's Organic & All Natural BBQ Sauces family.

The marinade is an extension of Tim's personal philosophy to have no secrets. "We don't keep anything from our customers and students," he says. "Our motto is: 'The answer is yes—what's the question?'" Tim considers it a great compliment if someone appreciates his cooking enough to ask for a recipe and he's always happy to share it.

Steve and Angel Cropper at cooking class.

The satisfaction he gets from sharing his love of cooking has allowed Chef Creehan to enter a new phase of his career—live cooking demonstrations and TV appearances. "I really enjoy doing live shows," he says. "At first it was a little intimidating, but now it is one of my favorite things to do. I can inject a little

Amy Grant assists Tim at cooking class.

humor, talk about current events and even employ a little drama when I'm teaching people about cooking.

"In 2003, I had a cooking class of 50 eager students in Nashville, Tennessee," Creehan recalls. "One of the most beautiful and talented assistant chefs I ever taught was in that class—Amy Grant. We had a blast! Amy is a natural cook. Her enthusiasm and passion for cooking was obvious. That's why I love to teach; I can see the pleasure and the excitement in my students' eyes. In fact, I think I could teach full time."

In 2002, *Country Weekly* magazine asked Tim to create a special dish for country music artist Tammy Cochran. "The tribute dish—Tammy's Fish Trio—was a resounding success," he recalls with satisfaction. "It's fun to work with celebrities," Creehan says. "While some expect the 'star treatment,' I have found most celebrities to be very down to earth. We have had some interesting requests from celebrities, but a lot of them are tired of people trying to outdo themselves to impress them. They are looking for simple comfort food and we're happy to oblige."

In 2000, entertainers Amy Grant and Vince Gill asked Chef Creehan if he would be the Chef de Cuisine for their wedding reception. In addition, other celebrities—Cybill Shepherd, Timothy Hutton, Debra Winger and Kathryn Crosby—have asked Creehan to serve as their personal chef.

In addition to preparing delicious meals for celebrities, Tim is thrilled to participate in cooking events and fundraisers. "It's really great to be able to give back to the community. We are always happy to help out. A large part of our marketing plan is to participate in events that promote Florida and the Florida Panhandle, known as the Emerald Coast. I'm delighted to be asked."

Tim loves being the owner and executive chef of his own restaurant. He freely admits that he loves what he does—every minute and every aspect of it. He thrives on challenges. "I love taking a raw product, and with my own two hands, turning it into something that gives others joy. I truly believe that I am one of the most fortunate chefs on the planet."

Tim Creehan is indeed "a fish that found water."

FROM THE CHEF

I have always tried to be ahead of the curve. Long before today's self-proclaimed lifestyle experts were calling for everyone to simplify, to scale back and make life less complicated, I was telling my friends, students and patrons that 'simple is good'—and that it was especially true when it came to preparing food. My philosophy can be summed up in one sentence: *Find the best and freshest ingredients you possibly can—then prepare them simply.*

While other boys were dreaming about becoming a baseball, basketball or football player, I was dreaming about becoming a chef. How did I know that at age 14, I had found my life's calling? I was very much influenced by my Uncle John Vignone, who was a chef, and then there were two generations of grandmothers—Vignone and Creehan—who cooked up a storm. So it was pretty much inevitable. Cooking was in my blood. Food and food preparation was a big part of all of our lives. Plus, I was incredibly fortunate to have been taken under the wing of world-renowned Executive Chef Philippe Parola.

My love of cooking flourished in my native Louisiana. Dinner in the Creehan household was sacred. Sundays after church it was always pasta or roast beef. When we visited family and friends in Connecticut, we were treated to New England and Italian cuisine. And when they visited us, my family spoiled them with delicious Southern Louisiana spreads. Almost every meal was prepared simply.

My earliest memories were of watching my mom, my grandmothers and my great grandmother cook. It didn't matter whose kitchen I was in—it was all about food! Naturally, I gravitated to the kitchen to find out how they made those delicious meals. Of course, it always looked like fun and the cook always seemed to be the most popular person in the house!

When I was looking for advice and direction, I took it upon myself to visit area restaurants. I was incredibly fortunate to meet Chef Parola, who was trained in Europe's finest traditions, schools, and kitchens. I will forever be in his debt! Chef Parola taught me so much, principles to live by and principles to cook by, some that I use every day, like this one: "Food's indigenous attributes should always speak for themselves."

As time passed and my confidence grew, I became more aware of how much cooking for my family and friends meant to me—and to them. For me, it's the total atmosphere—the food, flavors and textures—all of them bring fond memories flooding back. It's funny how much cooking can influence your entire life. I've cooked for lots of people over the years, some of them quite famous. I've created a lot of recipes and been recognized for my work, but when I need comfort food, I remember my childhood, and I do my best to re-create my family's simple recipes.

Cooking and entertaining are so much a part of my life that they have seamlessly blended into one of my other passions—sailing. The parallels may not seem obvious at first, but it's true. Sailing, like creating recipes, is an art form. With sailing you don't just turn the key and go; first you must understand the natural elements—the wind, the sea and the weather. You need a great deal of patience to adapt to these ever-changing elements, because the elements are certainly not going to change for you! The excitement is in the journey—not in the destination.

Sailing and creating recipes have a great deal in common. If you replace the wind, sea and weather with culture, ingredients and the environment, cooking is very much like sailing. It's often a challenge: you're given certain ingredients, some of which you may not be familiar with, or perhaps a culture that's completely foreign to you. Your challenge is to create something pleasing—not only to you— but to others as well. I'm in heaven when I can cook for my family and friends on my sailboat. In that moment, I can bring everything and everyone together that gives meaning to my life.

One way to share my joy of cooking is to keep it simple, with easy-to-find ingredients and recipes that are easy to prepare. Cooking shouldn't be like building the great pyramids; cooking should be easy, fun and exciting! That's how I chose the recipes for this book. Some came from family and friends, others came from clients and students, and a few even came from the movies. The common denominator is that others have enjoyed them and I have found them easy to prepare.

This cookbook is a prime example of my passion for sharing the creation of simple dishes. I do, however, harbor some minor reservations. Poring over a recipe on a printed page seems to me like a contradiction. True cooking isn't about memorizing someone else's recipe and following it to the letter. True cooking is the result of much testing and experimentation; I call it *food evolution*. I prefer to think of recipes as building blocks, not as hard-and-fast rules that intimidate you, making you afraid to experiment. Cooking is an art form; it involves feeling. Recipes have no emotion. By making each of these recipes unique, *you* provide the heart and *you* provide the soul.

So have fun with this cookbook. Go ahead! Make notes. Doodle on the pages. Spill sauce on your favorite recipe. Don't be afraid to have fun! I hope you will be inspired to create your own style, and that you will also become as passionate about the joy and the art of cooking as I am.

More than just a collection of recipes, this cookbook is a compilation of family history, traditions, and enjoyable times spent with guests, students and celebrities. I really appreciate it when someone shares a favorite recipe with me because I know how much time, creativity and care probably went into that recipe.

Each of us is part of a huge tapestry of shared experiences. Of this I am certain: I'm going to spend the rest of my life creating dishes for my family, friends, students and patrons . . .

It's that simple.

CHEF'S GRILL PLUS® INSTANT MARINADE

In the recipes that follow, you'll see references to Tim Creehan's Chef's Grill Plus Instant Marinade, a patented product that prevents foods from sticking to grill surfaces, as well as being a healthy alternative to butter and oil in baked, broiled or sautéed recipes.

Chef's Grill Plus is revolutionary! Simply brush it on, rub it on, or toss it with anything you want to grill, broil, bake or sauté. Chef's Grill Plus does the rest. No more sticking to the grill or dangerous flare-ups. The egg base, which contains very little oil, adheres to the food the second it gets hot, making it virtually nonstick instead of dripping onto the cooking surface. Chef's Grill Plus results in beautiful grill marks while imparting appetizing color to whatever you're cooking. Chef's Grill Plus is rapidly becoming a staple in everyone's kitchen.

Chef's Grill Plus was patented in the late 90's. It's not often that you see a food product get a patent, which confirms that we are changing the way people cook. In the process, we have taken heart health into consideration: this product is low in fat, sodium and cholesterol. Similar products and methods have two to three times more fat than Chef's Grill Plus!

While sugar is listed among the ingredients, it should not be a concern for people on a low-sugar diet. The only sugar in the recipe occurs naturally from one of the ingredients, not raw sugar.

There are several cost savings associated with Chef's Grill Plus. Unlike typical marinades, you only apply what you need directly to the food. There is little or no waste, and there's nothing to throw

out when you're finished. Also, the seasonings are already in the recipe, so you don't have that expense. In cost comparisons, Chef's Grill Plus cost 25-50% less than all other methods when preparing the same recipe. Last but not least, Chef's Grill Plus is cleaner and easier to use; you save both time and money on clean-up.

Paul Perfilio, National Marketing Manager for the National Pork Board said, "Chef's Grill Plus®
marinade brings out the best of any meat or seafood; it especially enhances the flavor of
grill-ready fresh pork. The 'nonstick' feature is an added-value benefit."

For more information and to order, see page 186.

SHRIMP SCAMPI PASTA

INGREDIENTS ———————————————————————— Serves 2

1/4 pound uncooked pasta	1/4 cup white wine (or water)
1/4 cup Herbs and Garlic Chef's Grill Plus	1/2 cup chopped tomato
1/2 pound (26 to 30-count) peeled shrimp	1 cup spinach
	grated Romano cheese to taste

METHOD

1. Cook the pasta using the package directions and drain. Set aside.

2. Heat the Chef's Grill Plus in a large sauté pan and add the shrimp. Sauté till the shrimp are curled and pink. Add the wine and tomato; cook 2 minutes.

3. Add the pasta and spinach; cook till heated through. Serve topped with cheese.

*The second I tasted Chef Creehan's
Grill Plus® sauce I knew it was going
to make cooking history; the flavor
was so explosive that it felt like my
taste buds were having a party!
Thank you for a wonderful new dining
experience.*
—Maddy Miller, Producer, CBS News

COCKTAILS

I was having some friends over for an intimate dinner. When they arrived, they were expecting stimulating conversation and, of course, a great dining experience. Before they sat down to enjoy the meal, I made a special effort to re-create an exotic cocktail from one of the many places I've visited during my travels. I presented the drink to my guests along with the story. The stage was set; now they were in the mood to savor and really enjoy the dinner. They sat back, relaxed and had the time of their lives. Mission accomplished!

Whether it is entertaining or dining out, I have always felt that everything should be the very best quality. Nothing should be second rate. The beverages you serve are no exception.

So when I travel, I make a special effort to get a feel for the local beverages. A few years ago, I sailed in the British Virgin Islands with some friends. We visited a famous beach bar called the Soggy Dollar on Jost Van Dyke. The specialty of the house was a local drink called the "Pain Killer." It captured the feel and mood of the islands perfectly. As soon as I returned to my restaurant, we added it to our list of specialty drinks. Occasionally we have a guest who can't believe we have it on our menu!

That's what I enjoy—surprising people, seeing them smile. I want our cocktails to "wow" people. That's why we use only the freshest ingredients to create—or re-create—drinks with the exact specs from all over the world. What a great way to make them feel at home.

DARK AND STORMY

INGREDIENTS ———————— Serves 1

3/4 ounce light rum
3/4 ounce dark rum
3/4 ounce fresh orange juice
3/4 ounce pineapple juice
3   ounces ginger beer
1   orange slice

METHOD

1. Combine the first 4 ingredients inside a shaker filled with ice.

2. Shake and strain into a tall beverage glass filled with ice. Slowly add the ginger beer. Garnish with an orange slice.

TAFFY APPLE

INGREDIENTS ———————— Serves 1

1 1/2 ounces vodka
3/4   ounce Apple Pucker sour apple liqueur
3/4   ounce butterscotch liqueur
       splash of sour mix
1/4   cup cinnamon
1   cherry

METHOD

1. Combine the first 4 ingredients inside a shaker filled with ice. Shake vigorously to mix.

2. Coat the rim of a martini glass with the cinnamon and strain the vodka mixture into the glass. Garnish with a cherry.

And do as adversaries do in law. Strive mightily, but eat and drink as friends.
—William Shakespeare

3 tsp = 1 tbsp • 2 tbsp = 1/8 cup • 4 tbsp = 1/4 cup • 5 tbsp = 1 tsp + 1/3 cup • 1 cup = 8 oz

DREAMSICLE

INGREDIENTS ———————— Serves 1

1¹/2	ounces vanilla vodka
1	ounce Cointreau
2	ounces fresh orange juice
¹/4	cup sugar
1	orange slice and Cherry Flag

METHOD

1. Combine the first 3 ingredients inside a shaker filled with ice. Shake vigorously to mix.

2. Coat the rim of a martini glass with the sugar. Strain the vodka mixture into the glass and garnish with an orange slice and cherry flag.

3. Cherry Flag: To create the cherry flag, split an orange and cut a slice into the orange running in the same direction as the segments, but not through the peel. Then turn the orange perpendicular to the slice and make 5 quarter-inch slices. Using a cocktail sword, insert a cherry onto the sword and stick the sword into the orange peel. This flag can now be placed on the edge of the glass using the slice cut down in its center.

RUM PUNCH

INGREDIENTS ———————— Serves 1

2	ounces Mount Gay rum
1	ounce pineapple juice
1	ounce guava juice
1	ounce fresh orange juice
¹/4	teaspoon freshly ground nutmeg
1	cherry

METHOD

1. Combine the first 4 ingredients inside a tall glass filled with ice. Mix well.

2. Garnish with a sprinkle of nutmeg and a cherry.

If more of us valued food and cheer and song above hoarded gold, it would be a merrier world.
—J.R.R. Tolkien

THE PAIN KILLER

INGREDIENTS ———————— Serves 1

2   ounces Pusser's rum
1   ounce fresh orange juice
1   ounce pineapple juice
1   ounce Coco Lopez
1/4 teaspoon freshly ground nutmeg
1   Cherry Flag (page 19)

METHOD

1. Combine the first 4 ingredients inside a shaker filled with ice; mix.

2. Pour into a tall glass and garnish with a sprinkle of nutmeg and a Cherry Flag.

When you go to the British Virgin Islands, you'll most likely run across the Soggy Dollar Bar on Jost Van Dyke where you can enjoy this libation. The Pain Killer is quite popular at most of the beach bars you may encounter. Here's our version.

ESPRESSO MARTINI

INGREDIENTS ———————— Serves 1

1   serving brewed espresso
1   ounce Godiva chocolate liqueur
3/4 ounce Kamora coffee liqueur
3/4 ounce Stolichnaya vanilla vodka
3   coffee beans

METHOD

1. Combine the first 4 ingredients inside a shaker filled with ice. Shake vigorously to mix.

2. Strain into a martini glass and garnish with coffee beans.

Eat not to dullness; drink not to elevation.
—Benjamin Franklin

3 tsp = 1 tbsp • 2 tbsp = 1/8 cup • 4 tbsp = 1/4 cup • 5 tbsp = 1 tsp + 1/3 cup • 1 cup = 8 oz

THE SHADY PEACH

1 1/2 ounces vodka
3/4 ounce peach schnapps
1 ounce fresh grapefruit juice
  splash of orange juice
1/4 cup sugar

METHOD

1. Combine the first 4 ingredients inside a shaker filled with ice. Shake vigorously to mix.

2. Sugar the rim of a martini glass.

3. Strain mixture into glass and garnish with an orange slice.

STARTINI

1 1/2 ounces vodka
2 ounces fresh lemonade
1/2 ounce Cointreau
  splash of Chambord
1 cherry

METHOD

1. Combine the first 4 ingredients inside a shaker filled with ice. Shake vigorously to mix.

2. Strain into a martini glass and garnish with a cherry.

Every man should eat and drink, and enjoy the good of all his labor; it is the gift of God.
—Ecclesiastes 3:13

APPETIZERS

Appetizers create anticipation for the guest. They inspire confidence in what's to come. A flavorful, artistically presented appetizer whets the appetite and all of the senses. A lasting impression is often the result of how the meal began, with a clever appetizer.

Preparation time for most appetizers is just a few minutes—the simpler the better!

Don't be afraid to experiment. Mix and match flavors, textures and seasonings. I, for one, have never been happy to leave well enough alone, especially when it comes to food. I call it *food evolution*; I'm always seeking something different. I want to make things better and I'm never afraid to try new things. For the most part, something new and exciting always comes from it. An example of this is my introduction to the Portabello mushroom.

About 15 years ago, a friend took me to a great Italian restaurant in Chicago. He had been there earlier and he knew there was something on the menu that I would really appreciate—the Portabello mushroom! Back then the Portabello mushroom had not become a household word. As always, my curiosity got the best of me. I tried it and I loved it! This versatile mushroom is visually and texturally rich and tastes very similar to steak. It is the perfect meat substitute. The mushroom offers an amazing array of possibilities. A loose translation of "Portabello" is "beautiful door." This intriguing mushroom does indeed open a beautiful door to exciting possibilities.

PORTABELLO MUSHROOM STACK

INGREDIENTS ——————————————————————————————— Serves 4

SAUCE

1 cup **Veal Stock** (page 134)
1/4 cup red wine
1 tablespoon butter

SPINACH STUFFING

1 tablespoon finely chopped bacon
2 tablespoons finely chopped
   yellow onion
1 cup spinach
   salt to taste
   black pepper to taste

MUSHROOMS

2 Portabello mushrooms
1 cup olive oil
1 teaspoon chopped garlic
   salt to taste
   black pepper to taste

ASSEMBLY

2 tablespoons warm goat cheese
8 chive stems (3-inch long)
2 teaspoons finely chopped
   red bell pepper

METHOD

1. For the sauce, combine the stock and wine in a saucepan. Bring to a simmer till reduced to the desired thickness. Add the butter and stir till melted. Keep warm.

2. For the mushrooms, clean and remove stems. Combine the oil, garlic, salt and pepper in a shallow dish. Add the mushrooms. Marinate the mushrooms till saturated with the marinade; drain. Place on a preheated grill surface and cook till tender. Cut into quarters.

3. For the stuffing, sauté the bacon and onion in a skillet till the onion is tender. Add the spinach and cook till the spinach is wilted. Season with salt and pepper.

4. For the assembly, spoon the spinach mixture evenly over four mushroom quarters. Place the 4 remaining mushroom quarters over the spinach. Spoon the sauce over the stacks. Spoon the goat cheese into a decorator tube. Pipe over the top of each stack. Garnish with chives and bell pepper.

3 tsp = 1 tbsp • 2 tbsp = 1/8 cup • 4 tbsp = 1/4 cup • 5 tbsp + 1 tsp = 1/3 cup • 1 cup = 8 oz

ESCARGOT WITH GARLIC BUTTER

INGREDIENTS ———————— Serves 4

24	French snails (96 count)
1/2	stick butter
1	tablespoon chopped garlic
2	tablespoons chopped parsley
	salt to taste
	white pepper to taste
	baked puff pastry pieces or
	toasted French bread slices
1	quartered lemon

METHOD

1. Sauté the snails with butter, garlic, parsley, salt and pepper in a large saucepan for 3 minutes. Spoon the mixture onto the puff pastry pieces on serving plates. Or, spoon onto serving plates; top with puff pastry. Garnish with lemon quarters.

Fresh snails are certainly an advantage, but good quality, small canned escargot are used in most cases. Snails baked in puff pastry are usually overdone; it is better to use the pastry or bread simply as a garnish.

GARLIC AND ALMOND BAKED BRIE

INGREDIENTS ———————— Serves 4

1/2	stick butter
1/2	cup sliced toasted almonds
1	teaspoon chopped garlic
2	tablespoons chopped parsley
	salt to taste
	black pepper to taste
1	Brie cheese (4-inch round)
1	sliced Granny Smith apple
	toasted bread slices

METHOD

1. Heat the butter in a sauté pan with the almonds and garlic. Add the parsley and season with salt and pepper.

2. Unwrap the Brie and heat in a microwave for 1 1/2 minutes. Pour the garlic-almond mixture over the Brie and serve with apple slices and toasted bread.

I never met a garlic I didn't like.
—Russ Russell

1/2 cup = 4 oz • 1 gal = 4 qts = 8 pts = 16 cups = 128 oz • 1 qt = 4 cups = 32 oz • 1 pt = 16 oz = 2 cups

MOZZARELLA BAKED GARLIC BREAD

1   loaf French bread
1   stick butter
2   tablespoons chopped garlic
1/4 cup chopped parsley
     salt to taste
     black pepper to taste
1/2 pound sliced Housemade Mozzarella (page 67)

METHOD

1.   Preheat oven to 500 degrees. Cut bread
     in half lengthwise. Melt the butter in a
     skillet and stir in the garlic and parsley.
     Brush over the cut sides of the bread.
     Sprinkle with salt and pepper.

2.   Place the bread on a baking sheet. Bake
     5 minutes or till golden brown. Top with
     mozzarella slices and bake till the cheese
     melts. Cut into slices and serve immediately.

MOZZARELLA WRAPPED IN ROMAINE

4   large romaine leaves
1/2 pound Housemade Mozzarella (page 67)
     salt to taste
     black pepper to taste
2   tablespoons grated Reggiano-Parmigiano
     cheese
1 1/2 cups warm Marinara Sauce (page 138)

METHOD

1.   Heat enough water to cover the romaine
     leaves in a saucepan. Add the romaine and
     wilt over low heat for 2 minutes; do not
     boil. Drain and let stand till cool.

2.   Cut the mozzarella into 4 pieces and season
     with salt and pepper. Place one piece of
     cheese on each romaine leaf and wrap
     the leaf to enclose the mozzarella.

3.   Heat in the oven or grill just till heated
     through. Place on a serving plate. Sprinkle
     with the Reggiano-Parmigiano cheese and
     serve with the Marinara Sauce.

Never eat more than you can lift.
—Miss Piggy

SUN-DRIED TOMATO BRUSCHETTA

INGREDIENTS ———————————— Serves 8

AÏOLI SAUCE

1/2	cup garlic cloves
1/2	cup Chicken Stock (page 130)
1	tablespoon olive oil
1/2	cup sour cream
	salt to taste
	white pepper to taste

BRUSCHETTA

16	slices Italian bread
3	tablespoons Herbs and Garlic Chef's Grill Plus
1/4	cup crumbled feta cheese
1/2	cup chopped Oven-Dried Tomatoes (page 80)
1/4	cup chopped basil

METHOD

1. For the aïoli, combine the garlic and Chicken Stock in a saucepan; cook till the garlic is tender. Drain, reserving the garlic. Sauté the garlic in the oil in a saucepan till brown. Combine with sour cream in a food processor; process till smooth. Combine with salt and pepper in a bowl; mix well.

2. For the bruschetta, preheat a grill surface. Cut bread into 2-inch squares. Brush lightly with Chef's Grill Plus. Place on the grill surface and grill till brown on both sides.

3. Top the bread with cheese, tomatoes and basil. Drizzle with Aïoli Sauce.

CARPACCIO WITH MAYTAG BLUE CHEESE AND PORT WINE ONIONS

INGREDIENTS ———————————— Serves 4

1	cup (1/4-inch) julienned red onions
1	cup ruby port wine
1	(8-ounce) sirloin strip steak
1/2	cup crumbled Maytag blue cheese
1/4	cup chopped chives

METHOD

1. Combine the onions and wine in a sauté pan; bring to a simmer. Simmer till the onions are tender and sauce is of a syrup consistency. Set aside.

2. Trim the steak and slice thinly. Place the slices on moistened plastic wrap and cover. Pound lightly with the flat side of a meat tenderizer. Arrange on a serving plate. Drizzle with syrup. Sprinkle with onions and cheese. Garnish with chives.

My favorite animal is steak.
—Fran Lebowitz

PORK SHO MAI

INGREDIENTS ———————————————————————————— Serves 4

1¹/₂ cups ground pork
1 tablespoon minced yellow onion
¹/₂ teaspoon minced pickled ginger
2 teaspoons minced green onions
1 teaspoon salt

white pepper to taste
pinch of minced garlic
1 egg white
20 round won ton wrappers (3-inch)
1 recipe Soy Dipping Sauce (page 139)

METHOD

1. Combine the first 8 ingredients in a bowl; mix well. Place 2 teaspoons of the mixture in the center of each wrapper. Bring the wrapper up around the filling and pleat the edge of the wrapper with your fingertips to form a straight-sided cup. Repeat with remaining filling. Chill for one hour or longer.

2. Steam in a traditional bamboo steamer for 4 minutes, or cook, covered, in a nonstick pan of boiling water one-inch deep. Serve with Soy Dipping Sauce.

This is a classical Chinese dim sum item like the Lobster Pot Stickers on page 30 and the Crab Meat Spring Rolls on the following page. The wrappers are usually filled with a variety of meats or seafoods. They are normally bite-size and round or elliptical in shape.

3 tsp = 1 tbsp • 2 tbsp = ¹/₈ cup • 4 tbsp = ¹/₄ cup • 5 tbsp + 1 tsp = ¹/₃ cup • 1 cup = 8 oz

CRAB MEAT SPRING ROLLS

2	ounces uncooked bean thread noodles	1/2	cup grated carrots
1	pound crab claw meat	2	teaspoons white pepper
2	cups thinly sliced Napa cabbage	20	spring roll wrappers
2	teaspoons finely chopped garlic	4	beaten egg yolks
1	bunch chopped green onions		peanut oil for deep-frying
		1	recipe Soy Dipping Sauce (page 139)

METHOD

1. Cover the noodles with cold water in a bowl. Let stand for 15 minutes; drain well. Combine with the next 6 ingredients; mix well.

2. Place one wrapper on a work surface with a corner pointing toward you. Place a full 1/4 cup of the crab meat mixture in the center of the wrapper and roll half way up starting at the bottom. Fold 1/3 of the side corners over the filling. Brush the remaining corner with the beaten egg yolks and finish rolling. Place in a deep pan lined with parchment paper. Repeat with the remaining ingredients, layering the spring rolls in the pan and placing parchment paper between the layers.

3. Heat the oil to 350 degrees in a deep fryer. Add the spring rolls a few at a time and fry 4 minutes or till golden brown. Serve immediately with Soy Dipping Sauce.

One must eat to live, and not live to eat.
—Jean Baptiste Moliere

1/2 cup = 4 oz • 1 gal = 4 qts = 8 pts = 16 cups = 128 oz • 1 qt = 4 cups = 32 oz • 1 pt = 16 oz = 2 cups

LOUISIANA BLUE CRAB CAKES

INGREDIENTS ———————————— Serves 12

3/4 cup Béchamel Sauce (page 136)
1/2 finely chopped yellow onion
1 tablespoon chopped garlic
1 tablespoon chopped parsley
1 teaspoon salt
1 teaspoon black pepper
2 cups homemade fine bread crumbs
1 pound jumbo lump crab meat
1/4 cup melted butter
1 recipe Grilled Vegetable Salsa (page 143)

METHOD

1. Preheat oven to 375 degrees. Combine the first 6 ingredients in a bowl; mix well. Add the crab meat and mix gently; do not break up the lumps of crab meat. Add one cup of the bread crumbs.

2. Divide into portions by spooning into a 3-ounce ladle and leveling the top. Roll each portion in the remaining one cup bread crumbs; shape each into a cake.

3. Place on a baking sheet brushed with melted butter. Bake for 10 minutes, turning once. Serve with Grilled Vegetable Salsa.

LOBSTER POT STICKERS

INGREDIENTS ———————————— Serves 4

1 cup chopped lobster meat
1/4 teaspoon chopped gingerroot
1/4 teaspoon chopped garlic
1 teaspoon chopped chives
  salt to taste
  white pepper to taste
20 won ton wrappers
1 quart water
2 tablespoons canola oil
1 recipe Soy Dipping Sauce (page 139)

METHOD

1. Combine the first 6 ingredients in a bowl; mix well. Spoon one heaping tablespoon of the mixture onto each won ton wrapper. Brush the outer edges of the wrappers with water. Fold one edge of each wrapper over the filling to form a half moon or triangle shape and press to seal. Repeat using the remaining filling.

2. Bring the water to a boil in a wok. Add the pot stickers and cook for 3 minutes; drain the water completely. Add the oil to the wok and heat. Let the potstickers lay on the flat side. Fry till golden brown. Serve immediately with Soy Dipping Sauce.

3 tsp = 1 tbsp • 2 tbsp = 1/8 cup • 4 tbsp = 1/4 cup • 5 tbsp + 1 tsp = 1/3 cup • 1 cup = 8 oz

BARBECUED SHRIMP WHOLE WHEAT QUESADILLAS

INGREDIENTS ———————————— Serves 4

1/2	pound boiled and peeled shrimp
1/2	cup barbecue sauce
4	(8-inch) whole wheat tortillas
1/2	pound shredded Cheddar cheese
1/2	pound shredded Monterey Jack cheese

METHOD

1. Preheat an oven broiler. Toss the shrimp in the barbecue sauce; set aside.

2. Lay the tortillas on a baking sheet. Top half with the Cheddar and half with the Monterey Jack. Spread the shrimp over the half topped with the Monterey Jack.

3. Broil till the cheese has melted. Marry the opposite pieces and press together. Broil on both sides to desired crispness. Cut into sixths. Serve immediately.

4. Serve with sour cream and Pico de Gallo on page 143 if desired.

Quesadillas are cooked many ways. Most sauté the tortillas in fat on a griddle. If you prefer oil or butter, the shells can be brushed prior to cooking.

THAI MUSSELS

INGREDIENTS ———————————— Serves 8

1	tablespoon butter
1	chopped yellow onion
1	tablespoon chopped garlic
1	seeded and chopped jalapeno
2	chopped tomatoes
1	tablespoon lime juice
1/2	bunch chopped cilantro
1/2	cup white wine
3	tablespoons tomato paste
160	mussels
1	(14-ounce) can coconut milk
	salt to taste
	black pepper to taste

METHOD

1. Combine the first 9 ingredients in a saucepan; bring to a boil. Add the mussels and cook till the shells open.

2. Add the coconut milk. Cook till the sauce is reduced to the desired consistency. Season with salt and pepper.

He who commands the sea has command of everything.
—Themistocles

GRILLED SEA SCALLOPS WITH KEY LIME SAUCE, CRISPY BACON AND TOMATO

1/2	cup heavy cream	16	large sea scallops
1/2	cup white wine	2	tablespoons Original Chef's Grill Plus
1/4	cup Key lime juice	1/2	cup chopped tomato
2	sticks butter	1/4	cup cooked crisp crumbled bacon
	salt to taste		
	white pepper to taste		

METHOD

1. Bring the cream, wine and lime juice to a boil in a heavy saucepan. Cook till reduced by half. Reduce the heat. Cut butter into small pieces. Add the butter to the sauce gradually, stirring till melted; do not boil. Season with salt and pepper.

2. Preheat the grill surface. Brush the scallops with Chef's Grill Plus and place on the grill rack. Grill to desired doneness.

3. Arrange the scallops on a plate. Top with wine sauce and garnish with tomato and bacon.

You don't have to cook fancy or complicated masterpieces—just good food from fresh ingredients.
—Julia Child

3 tsp = 1 tbsp • 2 tbsp = 1/8 cup • 4 tbsp = 1/4 cup • 5 tbsp + 1 tsp = 1/3 cup • 1 cup = 8 oz

JALAPENO HOLLANDAISE BAKED OYSTERS

1	cup Hollandaise Sauce (page 154)		1	teaspoon chopped garlic
1/2	finely chopped jalapeno			salt to taste
1	slice bacon, chopped			black pepper to taste
1/4	cup finely chopped onion		20	shucked oysters
2	cups fresh spinach			

METHOD

1. Preheat oven to 450 degrees. Combine the Hollandaise Sauce with the jalapeno in a bowl and set aside.

2. Sauté the bacon and onion till the bacon is crisp and the onion is tender. Add the spinach and garlic; cook till the spinach is wilted. Season with salt and pepper. Let stand till cool.

3. Place the oysters in an oyster dish or leave on the half shell and place on a baking dish. Spoon an equal amount of the spinach mixture onto each oyster. Bake 7 minutes. Arrange the oysters on a serving platter. Top with Hollandaise Sauce.

He was a bold man who first swallowed an oyster.
—King James I of England

JALAPENO AND GARLIC BREAD BAKED OYSTERS

INGREDIENTS ———————————— Serves 6

30	oysters on the half shell
3/4	cup homemade bread crumbs
I	stick melted butter
I	tablespoon chopped garlic
6	sprigs parsley
1/2	jalapeno
2	teaspoons salt
I	sliced lemon

METHOD

1. Preheat oven to 450 degrees. Place the oysters in an oyster dish or leave in the shell and place on a baking sheet. Sprinkle with bread crumbs. Purée the next 5 ingredients in a blender. Spoon over the oysters.

2. Bake 8 minutes. Place on a serving platter. Garnish with lemon slices. Serve immediately.

NEW ORLEANS STYLE BARBECUED SHRIMP

INGREDIENTS ———————————— Serves 4

32	(16 to 20-count) shrimp
2	sticks butter
1/4	cup Worcestershire sauce
I	tablespoon chopped garlic
2	teaspoons chopped fresh rosemary
I	teaspoon chopped fresh thyme
	salt to taste
I	tablespoon black pepper
I	teaspoon cayenne pepper
	warm toasted French bread

METHOD

1. Using kitchen shears, cut the shell of each shrimp along the top edge, leaving the shell on each shrimp.

2. Combine the next 8 ingredients in a large sauté pan. Simmer for 5 minutes. Add shrimp and cook to desired doneness.

3. Serve immediately with French bread for dipping.

Classic barbecued shrimp are prepared with the head on, cooked in the sauce. This adds flavor to the sauce and protects the flesh of the shrimp. The only drawback is that it is very difficult to eat this way. My dish utilizes the best of both worlds, removing the head and cutting the shell before cooking. They are then easily removed at the table, and the texture is the same as the classical preparation.

3 tsp = I tbsp • 2 tbsp = 1/8 cup • 4 tbsp = 1/4 cup • 5 tbsp + I tsp = 1/3 cup • I cup = 8 oz

GRILLED SHRIMP WITH CUMINO SAUCE

CUMINO SAUCE

1/2	cup white wine		1	chopped garlic clove
2	teaspoons lemon juice		1	cup canned peeled tomatoes with juice
1	teaspoon celery seeds		2	tablespoons flour
2	teaspoons ground cumin		2	tablespoons melted butter
1	tablespoon chopped shallots			salt to taste
2	cups heavy cream			cayenne pepper to taste
2	tablespoons chopped onion			

SHRIMP

24 (16-20 count) shrimp
3 tablespoons Original Chef's Grill Plus

METHOD

1. For the sauce, combine the first 9 ingredients in a saucepan. Bring to a boil and reduce by half the original volume.

2. Blend the flour and butter in a small bowl and stir into the sauce. Return to a boil, stirring till thickened and smooth. Reduce the heat and simmer for 20 minutes. Season with salt and pepper.

3. For the shrimp, preheat the grill surface. Brush the shrimp with Chef's Grill Plus and place on the grill. Grill the shrimp to desired doneness. Arrange on a serving plate and top with the Cumino Sauce.

This Cumino Sauce recipe was developed for a wonderful lady I worked for in Louisiana, Kacoo Olinde, co-founder of Ralph and Kacoo's Seafood Restaurants.

1/2 cup = 4 oz • 1 gal = 4 qts = 8 pts = 16 cups = 128 oz • 1 qt = 4 cups = 32 oz • 1 pt = 16 oz = 2 cups

SHRIMP FT. LAUDERDALE

1/4	stick butter		1	tablespoon tomato paste
1	teaspoon chopped garlic		1	cup heavy cream
18	(16-20 count) peeled and deveined Gulf shrimp		1/4	cup chopped parsley
				salt to taste
1	cup chopped tomato			white pepper to taste
1/4	cup white wine		3	cups cooked pasta or rice
2	tablespoons lemon juice		6	lemon wedges

METHOD

1. Melt the butter in a sauté pan. Add the garlic, shrimp and tomato; sauté briefly. Add the wine and lemon juice. Cook for 5 minutes. Stir in the tomato paste, cream and parsley; season with salt and pepper.

2. Cook till the sauce is reduced almost by half and coats the back of a spoon. Serve over cooked pasta or rice and garnish with lemon wedges.

While attending the Ft. Lauderdale boat show with my good friends Ed and Theresa Johnson, I was challenged to re-create a dish we enjoyed while visiting an Italian restaurant. I put my own twist on it and they loved it. Et voila: Shrimp Ft. Lauderdale!

MOZZARELLA AND ASPARAGUS STUFFED SHRIMP

6	steamed and chilled asparagus spears
12	slices Housemade Mozzarella (page 67)
12	(16-20 count) peeled and butterflied shrimp
12	slices pancetta
1/2	cup melted butter
3	tablespoons white wine
3	tablespoons lemon juice
1/4	cup bread crumbs
	black pepper to taste
3	tablespoons Romano cheese

METHOD

1. Preheat oven to 450 degrees. Split spears lengthwise and cut mozzarella into 1/4-inch by 1/4-inch by 2-inch slices. Place 1/2 asparagus spear and a piece of mozzarella in each shrimp and close the sides of the shrimp to enclose the filling. Wrap with pancetta. Arrange the shrimp in a baking pan.

2. Combine the butter, wine and lemon juice in a bowl and mix well. Pour over the shrimp. Sprinkle with the remaining ingredients. Bake for 7 minutes. Place on a serving platter; top with pan drippings.

Pancetta is an Italian bacon which is rolled. Unroll the sliced pancetta to make one long piece to wrap around the stuffed shrimp.

SHRIMP BUTTER

3	cups cooked (70-90 count) shrimp
1	stick butter at room temperature
8	ounces cream cheese at room temperature
1/2	cup sour cream
3/4	cup tomato paste
1	tablespoon lemon juice
1/2	cup finely chopped Vidalia or Maui onion
1	tablespoon finely chopped garlic
1/2	cup chopped parsley
1	tablespoon Crystal hot sauce
1	teaspoon Worcestershire sauce
1	teaspoon cayenne pepper
50	small gourmet crackers
2	tablespoons chopped parsley or chives

METHOD

1. Reserve 1/2 cup of the shrimp. Combine the next 11 ingredients with remaining shrimp in a food processor; mix well.

2. Spoon the shrimp butter into a pastry tube and pipe onto the gourmet crackers. Garnish with remaining shrimp, parsley or chives.

Option other than crackers: At the restaurant we cut sliced wheat toast with a one-inch round cutter and bake 7 minutes at 400 degrees.

1/2 cup = 4 oz • 1 gal = 4 qts = 8 pts = 16 cups = 128 oz • 1 qt = 4 cups = 32 oz • 1 pt = 16 oz = 2 cups

SOUPS

Often I am affected by something I see or hear that reinforces the wonderful memories I have about food and family. Some time ago there was a movie called, "Tortilla Soup." It was a great film; it embodied my whole philosophy of food, family and tradition. The film inspires you to go right to the kitchen and cook something. "Tortilla Soup," with all of its chopping, slicing and dicing, had that effect on me. I immediately headed for the kitchen to work on a new creation, Smoked Tomato and Shrimp Soup.

Soup is one of the few recipes in which improvisation is not only allowed; it is encouraged. I say, go straight to the refrigerator, open the door and see what's there, then create your own original soup. Don't worry if you've never tasted it before! It can be as individual as you are. And don't be concerned if the ingredients aren't at their peak. The nature of soup is that it has to cook anywhere from one-to-six hours. During this process it becomes one magical flavor. Enjoy the transition of flavors, and sample often. What could be simpler?

SMOKED TOMATO AND SHRIMP SOUP

2	yellow onions	1¹/2	quarts Chicken Stock (page 130)
4	tomatoes	1/4	cup sugar
1/3	pound chopped bacon	2	cups heavy cream
1/4	cup chopped garlic		salt to taste
3	cups canned Italian plum tomatoes		black pepper to taste
3	cups tomato sauce or purée	1	pound steamed (70-90 count) shrimp
1/2	cup tomato paste	1/4	cup chopped parsley or chive stems
2	canned chipotle peppers in adobo		

METHOD

1. Sprinkle a smoker with soaked hickory chips and preheat. Cut the onions in half and place them and the whole tomatoes on the smoker rack. Smoke over low heat for 30 minutes. Allow to cool and chop.

2. Sauté the bacon in a heavy soup pot. Add the onions, tomatoes and garlic. Cook for 15 minutes, stirring occasionally. Add the next 6 ingredients; mix well. Simmer for 20 minutes.

3. Process the mixture in batches in a blender or food processor till smooth. Combine the mixture in the soup pot; stir in the cream. Season with salt and pepper and heat to serving temperature. Ladle the soup into soup bowls and top with steamed shrimp and chopped parsley or chive stems.

Feel free to substitute the seafood of your choice in this versatile soup.

ASPARAGUS AND SUN-DRIED TOMATO SOUP WITH HERBED GOAT CHEESE

1	bunch asparagus	1/2	cup brandy
1	stick butter	1	quart Chicken Stock (page 130)
1	finely chopped yellow onion	2	cups heavy cream
1	finely chopped celery rib	1	tablespoon balsamic vinegar
1	tablespoon chopped garlic		salt to taste
1/2	cup flour		black pepper to taste
1	cup chopped sun-dried tomatoes	1/4	pound herb goat cheese

METHOD

1. Trim and chop the asparagus. Melt the butter in a soup pot. Add the onion, celery and garlic and sauté lightly. Stir in the flour and cook till bubbly. Add the next 4 ingredients. Bring to a boil, stirring constantly. Boil for 15 minutes.

2. Process the mixture in batches in a blender or food processor till smooth. Combine the batches in the soup pot and simmer for 15 minutes longer. Stir in the vinegar and season with salt and pepper.

3. Slice the cheese. Ladle the soup into soup bowls and garnish with cheese.

He ate and drank as he was told and
never let his soup get cold.
—Heinrich Hoffman

1/2 cup = 4 oz • 1 gal = 4 qts = 8 pts = 16 cups = 128 oz • 1 qt = 4 cups = 32 oz • 1 pt = 16 oz = 2 cups

PURÉE OF CHILI BEAN SOUP

4   cups chili beans without meat
2   cups tomato sauce
I   tablespoon chopped garlic
     chili powder to taste
     salt to taste
5   cups water
1/2 cup sour cream
I   recipe Pico de Gallo (page 143)

METHOD

1. Combine the first 3 ingredients in a saucepan. Cook till heated through. Purée the mixture with a hand mixer and season with chili powder and salt. Add enough water to make the desired consistency; heat to serving temperature.

2. Ladle the soup into bowls and garnish with sour cream and Pico de Gallo.

PORTABELLO, ONION AND BRIE SOUP

1/2 stick butter
4   cups chopped Portabello mushrooms
4   julienned Spanish onions
I   tablespoon chopped garlic
2   tablespoons sugar
2   cups red wine
2   quarts Veal Stock (page 134)
     salt to taste
     black pepper to taste
12   French bread croutons
12   thin slices Brie cheese
1/4 cup chopped green onions

METHOD

1. Melt the butter in a heavy soup pot. Add the mushrooms, onions and garlic. Sauté for 5 minutes. Add the sugar and cook till the onions are caramelized golden brown. Stir in the wine and Veal Stock. Bring to a boil and reduce the heat. Simmer for 30 minutes. Season with salt and pepper.

2. Preheat oven to 450 degrees. Arrange the croutons on a baking sheet. Top with the cheese. Toast just till the cheese melts.

3. Ladle into bowls and top with croutons. Garnish with green onions.

The success of this soup relies heavily upon a good fresh beef stock and the caramelization of the onions.

3 tsp = I tbsp • 2 tbsp = 1/8 cup • 4 tbsp = 1/4 cup • 5 tbsp = I tsp + 1/3 cup • I cup = 8 oz

BEAN, BUTTERNUT SQUASH AND CORN SOUP

2	tablespoons canola oil		1	pound butternut squash
2	cups chopped yellow onions		2	chopped tomatoes
2	chopped celery ribs		3	cups fresh or frozen corn kernels
2	chopped green bell peppers		1	(16-ounce) can Great Northern beans
1	tablespoon chopped chipotle pepper		6	chopped green onions
6	cups Chicken Stock (page 130)			salt to taste
2	bay leaves			black pepper to taste

METHOD

1. Heat the oil in a large soup pot over medium heat. Add the yellow onions, celery and bell peppers; sauté till the vegetables are golden brown, stirring occasionally. Add the chipotle pepper, Chicken Stock and bay leaves. Simmer for 30 minutes. Peel and chop the squash. Add the squash and the tomatoes. Cook for 45 minutes or till the squash is tender.

2. Add the corn, beans and 3/4 of the green onions. Simmer for 5 minutes or just till the corn is tender. Discard the bay leaves. Remove 3 cups of the soup and process in a blender or food processor till smooth. Combine with the remaining soup and heat to serving temperature. Season with salt and pepper.

3. Ladle the soup into bowls and garnish with the remaining green onions.

Too many cooks spoil the soup.
—Anonymous

1/2 cup = 4 oz • 1 gal = 4 qts = 8 pts = 16 cups = 128 oz • 1 qt = 4 cups = 32 oz • 1 pt = 16 oz = 2 cups

WAYNE'S PASTA AND BEAN SOUP

2	cups uncooked ditalini pasta		3/4	cup tomato sauce
1/2	pound ground pork		2 1/2	quarts water
1/2	finely chopped large onion		1	cup dried red beans
2	finely chopped celery ribs		1	cup dried white beans
1	cup grated carrot		1	teaspoon oregano leaves
1	tablespoon chopped garlic			salt to taste
6	cups Chicken Stock or Veal Stock			black pepper to taste
	(page 130 or 134)		10	teaspoons grated Romano cheese
1	cup canned crushed Italian plum tomatoes			

METHOD

1. Cook the pasta in a saucepan using package directions. Rinse and drain the pasta. Chill till serving time.

2. Brown the ground pork in a heavy soup pot, stirring till crumbly. Add the next 4 ingredients; sauté till the vegetables are tender. Add the Stock, tomatoes, tomato sauce, water, beans and oregano; mix well. Bring the mixture to a boil and reduce the heat. Simmer for 1 1/2 hours or till the beans are tender.

3. Season with salt and pepper. Ladle the soup into soup bowls and garnish with cooked pasta and cheese.

Of soup and love, the first is best.
—Spanish Proverb

3 tsp = 1 tbsp • 2 tbsp = 1/8 cup • 4 tbsp = 1/4 cup • 5 tbsp + 1 tsp = 1/3 cup • 1 cup = 8 oz

CHICKEN, CORN AND SWEET POTATO CHOWDER

1/2	pound butter	2	tablespoons balsamic vinegar
1	cup finely chopped onion	1	(12-ounce) can corn kernels
1/2	cup finely chopped celery	3	cups roasted chopped chicken
1/2	cup finely chopped carrot	2	cups heavy cream
3	cups chopped sweet potatoes	2	tablespoons finely chopped fresh basil
1/4	cup chopped garlic		salt to taste
1/2	cup flour		black pepper to taste
6	cups Chicken Stock (page 130)	1	cup chopped green onions
1	cup white wine		

METHOD

1. Melt the butter in a soup pot. Add the next 5 ingredients; sauté till the onion is translucent. Stir in the flour. Add the next 5 ingredients. Simmer for 15 minutes.

2. Stir in the cream, basil, salt and pepper. Simmer for 3 minutes. Ladle the soup into soup bowls and garnish with green onions.

This Bouillabaisse a noble dish is,
A sort of soup, or brothe or brew.
—William Makepeace Thackeray

1/2 cup = 4 oz • 1 gal = 4 qts = 8 pts = 16 cups = 128 oz • 1 qt = 4 cups = 32 oz • 1 pt = 16 oz = 2 cups

THAI CHICKEN SOUP

INGREDIENTS ———————————————————————— Serves 8

1/4	cup canola oil		3	tablespoons rice wine vinegar
2	chopped chicken breasts		1	cup quartered mushrooms
1	sliced yellow onion		2	tablespoons sugar
2	teaspoons chopped garlic		2	tablespoons chopped grated galanga
1/2	teaspoon chopped Thai chile peppers		3	kaffir lime leaves
2	stalks lemon grass			salt to taste
4	cups Chicken Stock (page 130)		1/4	bunch chopped cilantro
2	(13.5-ounce) cans coconut milk			

METHOD

1. Heat the oil in a soup pot. Add the chicken, onion, garlic and chile peppers; sauté briefly. Cut off the bottom 4 inches of the lemon grass stalks and add them to the pot with the next 8 ingredients.

2. Bring the mixture to a boil and remove from the heat immediately. Discard the lemon grass stalks and lime leaves. Ladle into soup bowls. Garnish with cilantro.

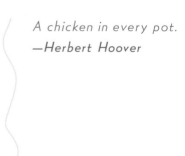

A chicken in every pot.
—Herbert Hoover

3 tsp = 1 tbsp • 2 tbsp = 1/8 cup • 4 tbsp = 1/4 cup • 5 tbsp + 1 tsp = 1/3 cup • 1 cup = 8 oz

GAZPACHO

INGREDIENTS ——————— Serves 8

1	chopped cucumber
1/2	chopped yellow onion
1/2	seeded chopped green bell pepper
1	garlic clove
1	quartered vine-ripened tomato
3	cups tomato sauce
4	cups Chicken Stock (page 130)
2	tablespoons red wine vinegar
	salt to taste
	freshly ground black pepper to taste
2	tablespoons chopped cilantro
2	tablespoons extra-virgin olive oil

METHOD

1. Reserve 1/2 cup of the cucumber for garnish. Combine the remaining cucumber and the next 7 ingredients in a food processor and process till smooth. Season with salt and pepper.

2. Chill one hour. Ladle into serving bowls. Garnish with reserved cucumber and cilantro. Drizzle with olive oil.

Gazpacho is a great summer soup.

PORTABELLO MUSHROOM CHILI

INGREDIENTS ——————— Serves 8

5	cups chopped Portabello mushroom caps
1	cup chopped yellow onion
2	teaspoons minced garlic
2	cups low-sodium tomato sauce
3	cups water
2	tablespoons chili powder
1	teaspoon ground cumin
1	teaspoon salt (optional)
	cayenne pepper to taste
1/4	cup shredded white Cheddar cheese
1/2	cup chopped red onion

METHOD

1. Combine the first 9 ingredients in a large soup pot. Bring to a boil and reduce the heat. Simmer for 20 to 25 minutes or till cooked to desired consistency, stirring occasionally.

2. Ladle the soup into bowls and garnish with cheese and red onion.

Soup of the evening, beautiful soup.
—Lewis Carroll

1/2 cup = 4 oz • 1 gal = 4 qts = 8 pts = 16 cups = 128 oz • 1 qt = 4 cups = 32 oz • 1 pt = 16 oz = 2 cups

ASSORTED MUSHROOM AND PANCETTA SOUP

1	stick butter	1	quart Chicken Stock (page 130)
1	cup chopped cooked pancetta	1	quart heavy cream
1	large finely chopped yellow onion	1/4	cup sherry
1	tablespoon chopped garlic	2	tablespoons lemon juice
2 1/2	pounds finely ground mixed Portabello,		salt to taste
	shiitake and oyster mushrooms		white pepper to taste
1	cup flour	1	cup chopped green onions

METHOD

1. Melt the butter in a heavy soup pot. Add the pancetta, yellow onion and garlic; sauté for 5 minutes. Add the mushrooms. Stir in the flour till all is incorporated. Reduce the heat.

2. Add the next 4 ingredients gradually, stirring constantly till smooth and thickened. Cook for 30 minutes, stirring occasionally to prevent sticking. Season with salt and pepper.

3. Ladle the soup into soup bowls and garnish with green onions.

An idealist is a man who looks at a rose, and thinks, because it smells sweet, it will make a better soup than a cabbage.
—H.L. Mencken

3 tsp = 1 tbsp • 2 tbsp = 1/8 cup • 4 tbsp = 1/4 cup • 5 tbsp + 1 tsp = 1/3 cup • 1 cup = 8 oz

TOMATO AND MUSHROOM CREAM SOUP

INGREDIENTS ——————————— Serves 8

1   stick butter
1   finely chopped yellow onion
2   finely chopped celery ribs
1   tablespoon chopped garlic
2   cups ground Portabello mushrooms
1   tablespoon chopped fresh rosemary
1/2 cup flour
2   cups milk
1   cup white wine
2   cups heavy cream
1 1/2 cups tomato sauce
     salt to taste
     black pepper to taste

METHOD

1.   Melt the butter in a heavy soup pot. Add the next 3 ingredients; sauté lightly. Stir in the mushrooms, rosemary and flour till all is incorporated.

2.   Add the next 4 ingredients and bring to a boil, stirring constantly till the mixture is thickened and smooth. Reduce heat and simmer for 30 minutes, stirring occasionally. Season with salt and pepper. Ladle into soup bowls.

ASPARAGUS AND CRAB MEAT SOUP

INGREDIENTS ——————————— Serves 8

1   stick butter
1   diced yellow onion
1   diced celery rib
1   tablespoon chopped garlic
1/3 cup white flour
1   cup white wine
2   cups milk
1   quart heavy cream
1   bunch chopped steamed asparagus
1/2 pound lump crab meat
     salt to taste
     black pepper to taste

METHOD

1.   Heat the butter in a stockpot. Add the next 3 ingredients; sauté briefly. Add the flour, stirring constantly till blended. Add the wine, milk and heavy cream; bring to a boil. Stir in the asparagus.

2.   Purée the soup in batches in a blender or food processor. Add the crab meat. Return soup to stockpot and simmer for 30 minutes. Season with salt and pepper.

This is a very versatile soup. Feel free to substitute the seafood of your liking.

POTATO AND CRAWFISH CHOWDER

1	stick butter	3	cups heavy cream
1	pound (peeled) crawfish tail meat	1	cup chopped blanched potatoes
1	finely chopped yellow onion	1/2	cup chopped green onions
1	tablespoon chopped garlic		juice of a lemon
2	teaspoons ground cumin	1	ounce sherry
1/4	cup flour		salt to taste
4	cups Chicken, Fish or Lobster Stock		black pepper to taste
	(pages 130, 132 or 133)		cayenne pepper to taste
1/4	cup tomato paste		

METHOD

1. Melt the butter in a heavy soup pot. Add the next 4 ingredients; sauté lightly. Stir in the flour till all is incorporated. Add the Stock, tomato paste and cream gradually, stirring occasionally. Bring to a boil.

2. Reduce the heat immediately and add the potatoes. Simmer for 30 minutes, stirring occasionally, or till the potatoes are tender. Add the green onions, lemon juice and sherry. Season with salt, black pepper and cayenne pepper. Ladle into soup bowls.

When the ship goes wop
  (with a wiggle between)
And the steward falls into the
  soup-tureen,
Why, then you will know
  (if you haven't guessed)
You're 'Fifty North and Forty West!'
—Rudyard Kipling

3 tsp = 1 tbsp • 2 tbsp = 1/8 cup • 4 tbsp = 1/4 cup • 5 tbsp + 1 tsp = 1/3 cup • 1 cup = 8 oz

BOILED SHRIMP BISQUE

INGREDIENTS ———————————— Serves 10

1	stick butter
1	large chopped yellow onion
1	tablespoon chopped garlic
1/4	cup flour
1	cup sherry
2	cups white wine
1	cup tomato paste
1	quart heavy cream
1 1/2	pounds boiled peeled (21-25 count) shrimp
	curry powder to taste
	salt to taste
	cayenne pepper to taste
1	cup chopped green onions

METHOD

1. Melt the butter in a heavy soup pot. Add the yellow onion and garlic; sauté for 5 minutes. Stir in the flour till all is incorporated.

2. Stir in the sherry, wine and tomato paste gradually. Add the cream and shrimp and bring to a boil, stirring occasionally.

3. Purée the mixture with a hand blender till smooth. Season with curry powder, salt and pepper.

4. Ladle the soup into soup bowls and garnish with green onions.

PUMPKIN BISQUE

INGREDIENTS ———————————— Serves 10

1	stick butter
1	chopped yellow onion
1	tablespoon chopped garlic
1	tablespoon flour
1	quart Chicken Stock (page 130)
1	quart heavy cream
1/2	cup dry sherry
4	cups canned or cooked fresh pumpkin
	sugar to taste
	salt to taste
	cayenne pepper to taste

METHOD

1. Melt the butter in a heavy soup pot. Add the onion and garlic; sauté till the onion is translucent. Stir in the flour and cook till bubbly. Stir in the Chicken Stock, cream and sherry gradually.

2. Add the pumpkin; mix well. Bring to a boil and reduce the heat. Simmer for 20 minutes. Season with the sugar, salt and pepper. Ladle into soup bowls.

1/2 cup = 4 oz • 1 gal = 4 qts = 8 pts = 16 cups = 128 oz • 1 qt = 4 cups = 32 oz • 1 pt = 16 oz = 2 cups

TORTILLA SOUP

INGREDIENTS ───────────────────────────────────── Serves 12

2	corn tortillas		1	chopped chipotle pepper
	oil for frying		1	teaspoon ground cumin
1/4	cup butter		1/4	cup chili powder
1	chopped yellow onion		1	cup heavy cream
1	teaspoon chopped garlic			salt to taste
3/4	cup masa harina		4	chopped green onions
2	quarts Chicken Stock (page 130)		1/2	chopped tomato
	juice of 1/2 lime			

METHOD

1. Cut the tortillas into thin strips and fry in oil in a skillet till crisp. Drain on paper towels and reserve.

2. Melt the butter in a heavy soup pot. Add the yellow onion and garlic; sauté for 5 minutes. Stir in the masa harina till blended well. Add the next 5 ingredients; mix well. Bring to a boil, stirring occasionally, and reduce the heat. Simmer for 20 minutes.

3. Process the mixture with a hand blender. Add the cream and mix well. Season with salt. Ladle into soup bowls and top with fried tortilla strips, green onions and tomato.

Some time ago, there was a movie called "Tortilla Soup." It was a great film; it embodied my whole philosophy of food, family and tradition. The film inspires you to go right to the kitchen and cook something.

3 tsp = 1 tbsp • 2 tbsp = 1/8 cup • 4 tbsp = 1/4 cup • 5 tbsp + 1 tsp = 1/3 cup • 1 cup = 8 oz

GRILLED ITALIAN SAUSAGE AND VEGETABLE SOUP

1/2 pound Italian sausage	2 quarts Chicken Stock (page 130)
1 pound assorted fresh vegetables of choice	2 cups canned or cooked dried white beans
1/3 cup Original Chef's Grill Plus	1 cup quartered mushrooms
1 tablespoon chopped garlic	1 tablespoon chopped fresh rosemary
2 chopped tomatoes	salt to taste
	freshly ground black pepper to taste

METHOD

1. Preheat the grill. Cut the sausage into halves lengthwise and place on the grill. Grill till cooked through and chop. Toss the assorted vegetables with the Chef's Grill Plus in a bowl. Grill till the vegetables are marked by the grill. Chop the vegetables.

2. Sauté the sausage with the garlic and tomatoes in a heavy soup pot for 5 minutes. Add the Chicken Stock, grilled vegetables, beans, mushrooms and rosemary; mix well. Cook for 45 minutes. Season with salt and pepper. Ladle into soup bowls.

Tomatoes and oregano make it Italian; wine and tarragon make it French. Sour cream makes it Russian; lemon and cinnamon make it Greek. Soy sauce makes it Chinese; garlic makes it good.
—Alice May Brock

1/2 cup = 4 oz • 1 gal = 4 qts = 8 pts = 16 cups = 128 oz • 1 qt = 4 cups = 32 oz • 1 pt = 16 oz = 2 cups

SALADS

I really enjoy thinking "outside the box" when I'm creating an original recipe. If for no other reason, it raises the bar of possibilities. I particularly enjoy experimenting with items that you would normally use in other preparations. My Asparagus Salad is one example of this philosophy.

Developing delicious lighter recipes has been a creative challenge. Over the last several years, I have been attuned to the growing trend of creating recipes that are simple to prepare, featuring ingredients that appeal to people interested in pursuing a healthy lifestyle. I like to highlight the main ingredient, such as chicken, with Asian, Thai and Japanese ingredients, instead of always relying on high-fat ingredients for flavor.

The editors of *Cooking Light*® magazine sponsored an event to recognize five chefs from all over the country. They chose one chef from each region, who in their opinion, achieved their mission of creating dishes that were light, healthy—and tasted great! *Cooking Light*® asked us to submit five recipes for consideration. They were especially pleased with my recipe for Thai Chicken Salad. After a few minor recipe adjustments, I was chosen—one of five Shining Star Chefs in the United States—for the GrandStand Event at Atlanta's Turner Field. In addition, we were all featured in *Cooking Light*® magazine and appeared at the Bolla Wines Shining Stars Café during the event. I enjoyed the entire experience. The attendance at the event was amazing—it was my largest audience yet!

ASPARAGUS SALAD WITH REGGIANO CREAM DRESSING

REGGIANO CREAM DRESSING

1¹/2 cups sour cream	1 cup grated Reggiano cheese
¹/2 cup red wine vinegar	black pepper to taste
1 tablespoon chopped garlic	

SALAD

8 slices pancetta	1 julienned red Roasted Sweet
40 medium stalks asparagus	Pepper (page 71)
8 green onions	

METHOD

1. For the dressing, combine the first 4 ingredients in a bowl; mix well. Season with black pepper. Chill till serving time.

2. Preheat oven to 350 degrees. Place the pancetta on a baking sheet and bake till crisp and brown; drain. Steam or boil the asparagus just till tender-crisp. Steam the green onions just till wilted. Arrange the asparagus stalks in bunches of 5 and tie each bunch with one green onion. Spoon the dressing onto 8 serving plates. Spread the asparagus stems apart at the base and stand in the dressing. Top with crisp pancetta and Roasted Sweet Pepper.

What garlic is to salad, insanity is to art.
—Augustus Saint-Gaudens

3 tsp = 1 tbsp • 2 tbsp = ¹/8 cup • 4 tbsp = ¹/4 cup • 5 tbsp + 1 tsp = ¹/3 cup • 1 cup = 8 oz

CORN, TOMATO AND ASIAGO CHEESE SALAD

INGREDIENTS ———————— Serves 6

3/4   cup fresh corn kernels
1/4   cup Regina red wine vinegar
1   tablespoon chopped garlic
1/2   chopped jalapeno
1/2   cup canola oil
      chili powder to taste
1   thickly sliced red onion
3   tablespoons Original Chef's Grill Plus
6   cups washed mixed baby greens
2   quartered vine-ripened tomatoes
1/2   cup shaved Asiago cheese

METHOD

1. For the dressing, combine the first 5 ingredients in a blender; mix well. Season with chili powder. Store chilled.

2. Preheat a grill surface. Brush the onion with the Chef's Grill Plus and cook till soft. Keep at room temperature.

3. Toss the mixed greens with the grilled onion and dressing. Garnish with tomatoes and cheese.

Fresh corn adds a great taste but don't miss this recipe if canned is all that is available.

ARUGULA AND PINE NUT SALAD

INGREDIENTS ———————— Serves 4

1/4   cup pine nuts
4   cups arugula
      juice of a lemon
2   tablespoons olive oil
1/4   cup shaved Reggiano cheese
      salt to taste
      freshly ground black pepper to taste

METHOD

1. Preheat oven to broil. Spread the pine nuts on a baking sheet and toast till golden brown. Sprinkle with salt.

2. Place the arugula in a bowl and drizzle with the lemon juice and oil. Toss to coat well. Spoon onto plates and top with cheese and pepper.

You need to have the soul of a rabbit to eat lettuce as it is usually served . . . A salad is only a background; it needs embroidering.
—Paul Reboux

1/2 cup = 4 oz • 1 gal = 4 qts = 8 pts = 16 cups = 128 oz • 1 qt = 4 cups = 32 oz • 1 pt = 16 oz = 2 cups

CURRIED LEMON CAESAR SALAD

LEMON CAESAR DRESSING

2	egg yolks	1	tablespoon Worcestershire sauce
1	tablespoon Dijon mustard	2	tablespoons lemon juice
1	teaspoon ground anchovy	1/4	cup red wine vinegar
1	tablespoon chopped garlic	1	cup extra-virgin olive oil

SALAD

1/2	head romaine lettuce	3/4	cup grated Romano cheese
1	bunch spinach	2	tablespoons curry powder
1	cup sliced mushrooms		freshly ground black pepper to taste
1	cup shaved carrots		

METHOD

1. For the dressing, combine the first 7 ingredients in a mixing bowl. Add oil gradually, whisking constantly till the mixture is thick and smooth. Chill till serving time.

2. For the salad, combine the first 4 ingredients in a bowl; toss to mix well. Chill till serving time.

3. Drizzle the dressing over the salad and sprinkle with the cheese and curry powder; toss to mix well. Serve immediately with pepper.

Our Garrick's a salad; for in him we see oil, vinegar, sugar, and saltiness agree!
—Oliver Goldsmith

3 tsp = 1 tbsp • 2 tbsp = 1/8 cup • 4 tbsp = 1/4 cup • 5 tbsp + 1 tsp = 1/3 cup • 1 cup = 8 oz

GRILLED EGGPLANT AND ROASTED PEPPER SALAD
WITH GOAT CHEESE

BALSAMIC VINAIGRETTE

1/2	cup extra-virgin olive oil	I	tablespoon chopped fresh basil
3	tablespoons balsamic vinegar		salt to taste
2	teaspoons chopped garlic		black pepper to taste

SALAD

4	red Roasted Sweet Peppers (page 71)		kosher salt to taste
I	eggplant		black pepper to taste
1/2	cup pomace olive oil	1/2	cup crumbled goat cheese

METHOD

1. For the vinaigrette, combine the first 4 ingredients in a bowl; whisk till smooth. Season with salt and pepper.

2. For the salad, see Roasted Sweet Peppers recipe. Julienne the peppers.

3. Preheat the grill. Cut the unpeeled eggplant lengthwise into thin slices. Brush with the oil and season with salt and pepper. Grill till tender; cut into strips.

4. Toss the Roasted Sweet Peppers and eggplant with the vinaigrette in a bowl. Chill in the refrigerator for 30 minutes. Spoon onto serving plates and top with cheese.

Olives and artichokes are also good additions to this salad.

1/2 cup = 4 oz • I gal = 4 qts = 8 pts = 16 cups = 128 oz • I qt = 4 cups = 32 oz • I pt = 16 oz = 2 cups

SENSATION SALAD

SENSATION DRESSING

1/4	cup olive oil		2	dashes Tabasco sauce
1/4	cup canola oil		1	tablespoon chopped red bell pepper
1/4	cup white vinegar		1/4	cup grated Romano cheese
1/4	cup lemon juice			salt to taste
1	tablespoon chopped garlic			white pepper to taste

SALAD

1/2	head chopped romaine		24	cherry tomatoes
1/2	head chopped iceberg lettuce		1/2	cup grated Romano cheese

METHOD

1. For the dressing, combine the first 6 ingredients in a mixing bowl. Add the next 4 ingredients; mix well. Chill till serving time.

2. For the salad, combine the romaine and iceberg lettuce in a bowl. Add the dressing and toss to mix well. Spoon onto serving plates and top with tomatoes and cheese.

Sensation Salad contains flavors very similar to those found in a classic Caesar salad, but is much lighter overall.

3 tsp = 1 tbsp • 2 tbsp = 1/8 cup • 4 tbsp = 1/4 cup • 5 tbsp + 1 tsp = 1/3 cup • 1 cup = 8 oz

BLUE CHEESE WEDGE

INGREDIENTS ——————————————— Serves 4

BLUE CHEESE DRESSING
1	cup mayonnaise
1	cup sour cream
1/4	cup red wine vinegar
1	teaspoon finely chopped garlic
1 1/2	cups crumbled blue cheese
1	teaspoon salt
1	teaspoon black pepper

SALAD
1	head iceberg lettuce
1/2	finely chopped red onion
4	thin slices pancetta
2	finely chopped tomatoes

METHOD

1. For the dressing, combine the first 4 ingredients in a medium mixing bowl; mix well.

2. Add the cheese, salt and pepper and mix gently. Store in the refrigerator till serving time.

3. For the salad, quarter the lettuce into wedges. Preheat oven to 350 degrees. Place the pancetta on a baking sheet and bake till crisp and brown.

4. Place one wedge on each serving plate. Spoon dressing over the wedges and sprinkle tomatoes and onion around edges. Top with a crisp pancetta slice.

WARM SPINACH SALAD

INGREDIENTS ——————————————— Serves 6

SALAD
4	cups packed spinach leaves
1	boiled and grated or sliced egg
1/4	cup sliced red Roasted Sweet Peppers (page 71)

HONEY MUSHROOM DRESSING
1	tablespoon chopped and cooked pancetta or prosciutto
1/3	cup honey
1/2	cup red wine vinegar
3/4	cup canola oil
1	cup sliced mushrooms

METHOD

1. For the salad, divide the spinach among 6 serving plates. Sprinkle with the egg and Roasted Sweet Peppers.

2. For the dressing, combine the first 4 ingredients in a blender; process till smooth. Combine with the mushrooms in a microwave-safe bowl. Microwave for 2 minutes. Spoon over the salads and serve immediately.

Gave up spinach for Lent.
—F. Scott Fitzgerald

1/2 cup = 4 oz • 1 gal = 4 qts = 8 pts = 16 cups = 128 oz • 1 qt = 4 cups = 32 oz • 1 pt = 16 oz = 2 cups

ASSORTED TOMATO SALAD

SHALLOT AND GARLIC VINAIGRETTE

1/2 cup sliced shiitake mushroom caps

2 tablespoons chopped shallots

1 teaspoon chopped garlic

1/2 cup crumbled feta cheese

1/2 cup red wine vinegar

2 teaspoons kosher salt

1/2 cup extra-virgin olive oil

1/4 cup canola oil

freshly ground black pepper to taste

SALAD

2 pounds assorted tomatoes of all sizes and colors

1 chopped cucumber

8 fresh basil leaves, chopped

METHOD

1. For the vinaigrette, combine the first 4 ingredients in a bowl. Add the vinegar and salt and let stand for 10 minutes. Add the olive oil and canola oil and season with pepper; mix well.

2. For the salad, cut the larger tomatoes into bite-size pieces. Combine the tomatoes in a salad bowl and toss to mix. Chill till serving time.

3. Add the vinaigrette to the tomato mixture and toss to mix well. Spoon onto serving plates and top with cucumber and basil.

The more sizes and colors of tomatoes, the better. Smaller tomatoes can be left whole; larger tomatoes can be cut into bite-size pieces.

ROASTED CHICKEN AND ARTICHOKE GREEK SALAD

4	cups quartered artichoke hearts
1	cup red bell pepper strips
1/2	cup chopped green onions
1	julienned yellow onion
2	peeled and sliced cucumbers
2	tablespoons chopped garlic
2	cups crumbled feta cheese
1	cup olive oil

1/2	cup white vinegar
1/4	cup lemon juice
	salt to taste
	black pepper to taste
5	cups roasted and pulled chicken
1/4	cup chopped kalamata olives
4	cups mixed greens (optional)

METHOD

1. Combine the first 7 ingredients in a large salad bowl. Combine the oil, vinegar and lemon juice in a small bowl. Pour over the salad and toss to mix well. Season with salt and pepper.

2. Add the chicken to the salad and mix gently. Top with the olives. Serve from the salad bowl or spoon onto plates lined with mixed greens.

*It's certain that fine women eat
a crazy salad with their meat.*
—William Butler Yeats

1/2 cup = 4 oz • 1 gal = 4 qts = 8 pts = 16 cups = 128 oz • 1 qt = 4 cups = 32 oz • 1 pt = 16 oz = 2 cups

WEST INDIES CRAB MEAT SALAD

INGREDIENTS ———————————— Serves 4

OLIVE DRESSING

1/2	quartered yellow onion
1/2	cup salad olives
2	teaspoons chopped garlic
1	cup canola oil
1/3	cup Regina red wine vinegar
	freshly ground black pepper to taste

SALAD

3	cups salad greens
1/2	pound lump crab meat
16	grape tomatoes
1/4	cup grated Romano cheese
4	lemon wedges

METHOD

1. For the dressing, combine the first 3 ingredients in a food processor; process till ground well. Combine with oil, vinegar and pepper in a bowl; mix well. Chill in refrigerator.

2. For the salad, toss greens and crab meat in a bowl. Add dressing and toss to coat well. Spoon onto plates and garnish with tomatoes, cheese and lemon wedges.

GRILLED ROMAINE AND LOUISIANA CRAWFISH SALAD

INGREDIENTS ———————————— Serves 4

1/4	minced onion
1	minced celery rib
1	tablespoon minced green bell pepper
1	minced garlic clove
1/4	pound butter
2	tablespoons brandy
1/2	cup Chicken Stock (page 130)
	juice of a lemon
	black pepper to taste
1	head romaine
1/2	pound (peeled) crawfish tail meat
1	cup crumbled blue cheese

METHOD

1. Sauté the first 4 ingredients in the butter for 5 minutes. Add the brandy and flambé. Cook till flames subside. Add the Chicken Stock and lemon juice; season with pepper. Keep warm.

2. Preheat a grill surface. Quarter the romaine, leaving the core attached. Place the romaine on the grill just till wilted; transfer to serving plates.

3. Add the crawfish to the vegetable mixture and cook just till heated through. Spoon over the romaine and top with cheese.

LOBSTER SALAD WITH A LATIN-STYLE VINAIGRETTE

LATIN VINAIGRETTE

1	egg yolk		juice of 2 limes
2	tablespoons brown sugar	1	tablespoon ground cumin
1/2	chipotle pepper in adobo		salt to taste
2	tablespoons chopped cilantro	1	cup canola oil
1	tablespoon red wine vinegar		

SALAD

6	cups mixed greens	2	cups chilled lobster meat
1/2	cup cooked and chilled black beans	32	halved grape tomatoes
1/2	cup sliced hearts of palm		

METHOD

1. For the vinaigrette, combine the first 8 ingredients in a blender; process till smooth. Add the oil gradually, processing constantly till well mixed. Chill till serving time.

2. For the salad, combine the first 4 ingredients in a bowl and mix gently. Add the desired amount of vinaigrette and toss to coat well. Spoon onto plates and top with tomatoes.

Let first the onion flourish there,
Rose among roots, the maiden-fair,
Wine-scented and poetic soul
Of the capacious salad bowl.
—Robert Louis Stevenson

1/2 cup = 4 oz • 1 gal = 4 qts = 8 pts = 16 cups = 128 oz • 1 qt = 4 cups = 32 oz • 1 pt = 16 oz = 2 cups

LOBSTER AND ASPARAGUS SALAD WITH TROPICAL FRUIT VINAIGRETTE

INGREDIENTS ———————————————————————— Serves 8

TROPICAL FRUIT VINAIGRETTE

1/4	cantaloupe, chopped	2	egg yolks
4	strawberries	1	cup canola oil
1/3	cup pineapple juice	1/4	bunch cilantro, chopped
1/4	cup mango juice		salt to taste
3/4	cup rice vinegar		black pepper to taste

SALAD

16	asparagus spears	6	cups mixed greens
3	ears fresh corn	32	halved grape tomatoes
3	cups steamed and chilled lobster meat		

METHOD

1. For the dressing, combine the first 6 ingredients in a mixing bowl; purée with a hand mixer or hand blender. Add the oil gradually, mixing constantly till well mixed. Stir in the cilantro and season with salt and pepper.

2. For the salad, split the asparagus spears lengthwise and steam till tender-crisp. Cover the corn with water in a saucepan; cook just till tender. Chill the asparagus and corn. Cut the corn off the cob. Combine the chilled vegetables with the lobster meat, mixed greens and desired amount of dressing in a bowl; mix well.

3. Divide the prepared salad among serving plates. Garnish with tomatoes.

What good are vitamins? Eat four lobsters, eat a pound of caviar—live!
—Arthur Rubenstein

3 tsp = 1 tbsp • 2 tbsp = 1/8 cup • 4 tbsp = 1/4 cup • 5 tbsp + 1 tsp = 1/3 cup • 1 cup = 8 oz

HOUSEMADE MOZZARELLA

INGREDIENTS ——————— Makes about 2 pounds

2   pounds mozzarella curd
3   quarts water
1/2 cup salt
     pinch of white pepper
1   quart milk
1   quart water
2   cups ice cubes

METHOD

1. Crumble the curd into a large bowl. Combine 3 quarts water, salt and pepper in a stockpot and bring to a rolling boil. Pour over the curd. Stir till the curd melts and begins to form strands. Remove 6 to 8 ounces and fold inward till it appears smooth and glossy. Do not overwork.

2. Make a brine by combining the milk, one quart water and ice cubes. Drop the pieces of curd into the brine till completely cool. Remove and wrap each piece individually. Keep refrigerated. Serve at room temperature.

GINGER VINAIGRETTE

INGREDIENTS——————— Makes 1 1/2 cups

2   tablespoons pickled gingerroot
2   tablespoons chopped garlic
5   finely chopped green onions
1/4 cup chopped cilantro
1/4 cup canola oil
1/4 cup lemon juice
2   tablespoons rice vinegar
2   tablespoons sugar
     salt to taste
     black pepper to taste

METHOD

1. Combine the first 4 ingredients in a food processor or blender. Add the next 4 ingredients; process till smooth. Season with salt and pepper.

2. Spoon into a container and chill for one hour or longer. Store, covered, in the refrigerator.

My salad days, when I was green in judgment.
—William Shakespeare

VEGETABLES & SIDES

Vegetables and side dishes are often the Rodney Dangerfield of cuisine—they get no respect. This is definitely not the case when I'm cooking; vegetables and side dishes have earned a respected place in my cuisine. Vegetables and side dishes can add immeasurably to the taste and success of a great meal.

Vegetables are, without a doubt, healthy. They are also appetizing, simple to prepare and incredibly versatile. Steaming, roasting, grilling, sautéing, baking—the ways to prepare a delicious vegetable or side dish are unlimited.

When I'm selecting the best vegetable or side dish to complement a particular recipe, I make sure that the taste, color and texture of the vegetables enhance not only the primary ingredient, but also the sauces I've prepared for the recipe. For example, I sauté fresh corn and serve it with fried lobster. Or I prepare mashed sweet potatoes with venison, or braised bok choy with roast duck. When you feel a recipe just needs a little more taste or texture, focus on the accompaniments. The possibilities are limited only by your imagination.

SWEET POTATO MASH · ROASTED GARLIC · SAUTÉED FRESH CORN
GRILLED ASPARAGUS · ROASTED SWEET PEPPERS · TOBACCO ONIONS · BRAISED BOK CHOY

GRILLED ASPARAGUS

INGREDIENTS ───────────── Serves 4

1	tablespoon baking soda
1	gallon water
20	medium stalks asparagus
3	tablespoons Original Chef's Grill Plus

METHOD

1. To boil the asparagus, combine the baking soda with one gallon of water in a large saucepan and bring to a boil. For smaller stalks, boil one minute; for larger stalks, boil 2 to 3 minutes. Plunge into ice water immediately to cool.

2. Preheat the grill. Brush the asparagus with the Chef's Grill Plus. Grill to desired doneness. Serve immediately.

BRAISED BOK CHOY

INGREDIENTS ───────────── Serves 8

1	head bok choy
1/4	cup canola oil
1	tablespoon chopped garlic
3/4	cup Chicken Stock (page 130)
1/4	cup soy sauce
	black pepper to taste

METHOD

1. Cut the bok choy into 1/4-inch pieces.

2. Heat a wok and add the bok choy, oil and garlic; stir-fry lightly. Add the Chicken Stock and soy sauce. Cook over high heat for 5 minutes. Season with pepper and serve immediately.

Never trust a dog to watch your food.
—Patrick, age 10, in Advice from Kids

3 tsp = 1 tbsp • 2 tbsp = 1/8 cup • 4 tbsp = 1/4 cup • 5 tbsp + 1 tsp = 1/3 cup • 1 cup = 8 oz

SAUTÉED FRESH CORN
OFF THE COB

ROASTED SWEET PEPPERS

INGREDIENTS ———————— Serves 4

4	ears fresh corn
2	tablespoons butter
I	teaspoon chopped garlic
	salt to taste
	black pepper to taste
I	tablespoon chopped parsley

INGREDIENTS ———————— Serves 4

6	red or gold peppers
1/2	cup extra-virgin olive oil
2	tablespoons Regina red wine vinegar
I	sprig chopped fresh parsley
I	clove chopped garlic
	salt to taste
	black pepper to taste

METHOD

1. Bring a large saucepan of water to a boil and add the corn. Cook for 12 minutes or till the corn is tender. Plunge into ice water to cool. Cut the kernels from the cobs.

2. Melt the butter in a sauté pan. Add the garlic and corn; sauté till the corn is heated through. Season with salt and pepper. Spoon into a serving bowl and garnish with parsley.

METHOD

1. Completely burn the skins of the peppers using a hot grill, open flame or torch. Rinse the skins off under cold running water. Pull off and discard the top stem and seeds. Tear into quarters.

2. Mix the next 6 ingredients in a bowl. Add peppers and marinate in the refrigerator for 30 minutes. Serve immediately or store in the refrigerator.

There are many methods of removing the skins from charred peppers, but I think the easiest and most effective is to wash them under cold water.

1/2 cup = 4 oz • I gal = 4 qts = 8 pts = 16 cups = 128 oz • I qt = 4 cups = 32 oz • I pt = 16 oz = 2 cups

ROASTED GARLIC

2   pounds kosher salt
10   whole garlic bulbs

METHOD

1. Preheat oven to 350 degrees. Cover the bottom of a small baking dish with some of the salt. Arrange the garlic bulbs flat side down in the salt and cover completely with the remaining salt.

2. Cover the dish with foil and bake for 45 minutes, or till tender but not dry. Split the bulbs horizontally.

Prepared garlic pods can be kept in the refrigerator and warmed in the oven or microwaved as needed.

TOBACCO ONIONS

1   medium onion
4   cups canola oil

METHOD

1. Cut the onion into very thin slices and separate into rings. Preheat the oil to 350 degrees in a large saucepan.

2. Add the onion rings to the hot oil; fry for 20 seconds or till dark brown. Place on a cloth or paper towel to drain till crisp.

A well-governed appetite is a great part of liberty.
—*Lucius Annaeus Seneca*

GREEN BEANS WITH PANCETTA AND ONIONS

INGREDIENTS ———————————— Serves 8

1	pound fresh green beans
2	quarts water
1/2	stick butter
1	cup chopped pancetta
1	large julienned yellow onion
1/2	cup Chicken Stock (page 130)
	kosher salt to taste
	black pepper to taste

METHOD

1. Blanch the green beans in water, just till tender-crisp; drain. Melt the butter in a large sauté pan. Add the pancetta and the onion; sauté till brown.

2. Add the beans and Chicken Stock to the sauté pan; season with salt and pepper. Cook just till the beans are heated through. Serve immediately.

SAUTÉED BABY GREEN BEANS

INGREDIENTS ———————————— Serves 4

1	quart water
40	fresh baby green beans (haricots verts)
1	tablespoon butter
	chopped garlic to taste
	salt to taste
	black pepper to taste

METHOD

1. Bring the water to a boil in a medium saucepan and add the beans. Blanch just till tender-crisp and drain.

2. Melt the butter in a large sauté pan; add the beans and garlic. Sauté just till heated through. Season with salt and pepper.

I was determined to know beans.
—Henry David Thoreau

1/2 cup = 4 oz • 1 gal = 4 qts = 8 pts = 16 cups = 128 oz • 1 qt = 4 cups = 32 oz • 1 pt = 16 oz = 2 cups

SWEET POTATO MASH

1¹/2   pounds sweet potatoes
¹/2   stick butter
¹/2   cup heavy cream
     salt to taste
     black pepper to taste

METHOD

1.   Peel and chop the potatoes. Cover the potatoes with water in a saucepan; cook till tender. Drain. Remove to a mixing bowl. Add butter, cream, salt and pepper; beat till smooth.

BRAISED BEAN SPROUTS

¹/4   cup canola oil
1   julienned yellow onion
     pinch of chopped garlic
5   cups bean sprouts
1   bunch chopped green onions
¹/4   cup soy sauce
     black pepper to taste

METHOD

1.   Heat a large sauté pan or wok. Add the oil, yellow onion and garlic; sauté lightly.

2.   Add bean sprouts and green onions. Sauté over high heat just till heated through. Season with soy sauce and pepper.

There is no love sincerer than the love of food.
—George Bernard Shaw

CREOLE COLE SLAW

1   cup mayonnaise
1/2   cup ketchup
1/4   cup white vinegar
1   tablespoon prepared mustard
1   teaspoon Worcestershire sauce
1/4   cup sugar
       salt to taste
       cayenne pepper to taste
1   cup shaved carrots
6   cups shredded green cabbage

METHOD

1. Combine the first 8 ingredients in a bowl and mix well.

2. In a separate bowl, mix the carrots and cabbage. Drizzle with the dressing mixture; toss to coat well. Refrigerate till serving time.

WHITE BEAN AND TRUFFLE OIL MASH

1   cup dried Great Northern white beans
3   quarts water
1   teaspoon chopped garlic
1   teaspoon salt
1/4   cup (or to taste) white truffle oil
       freshly ground black pepper to taste

METHOD

1. Combine the first 4 ingredients in a large saucepan; bring to a boil. Reduce heat and cook for 1 1/2 hours or till beans are very tender.

2. Process the mixture with the cooking liquid in a food processor till smooth. Drizzle in the truffle oil and mix well. Season with pepper.

When women are depressed, they either eat or go shopping. Men invade another country. It's a whole different way of thinking.
—Elaine Boosler

1/2 cup = 4 oz • 1 gal = 4 qts = 8 pts = 16 cups = 128 oz • 1 qt = 4 cups = 32 oz • 1 pt = 16 oz = 2 cups

ASSORTED GARLIC MUSHROOMS

MASHED PARSNIPS

INGREDIENTS ———————— Serves 6

1/4	stick butter
2	teaspoons chopped garlic
3	tablespoons chopped parsley
	salt to taste
	black pepper to taste
1	large sliced Portabello mushroom
2	cups sliced shiitake mushrooms
2	cups sliced domestic mushrooms

METHOD

1. Combine the first 5 ingredients in a large sauté pan. Heat till the butter melts, stirring to mix well.

2. Add mushrooms and sauté till tender. Serve immediately or keep warm till serving time.

INGREDIENTS ———————— Serves 8

3	pounds parsnips
1	cup heavy cream
2	cups milk
2	tablespoons chopped garlic
	salt to taste
	black pepper to taste

METHOD

1. Peel and chop parsnips. In a medium saucepan, cover with water and cook till tender; drain.

2. Add remaining ingredients; mix till smooth with a hand mixer.

If you reject the food, ignore the customs, fear the religion and avoid the people, you might better stay home.
—James Michener

3 tsp = 1 tbsp • 2 tbsp = 1/8 cup • 4 tbsp = 1/4 cup • 5 tbsp + 1 tsp = 1/3 cup • 1 cup = 8 oz

BROCCOLI AND PANCETTA MASHED POTATOES

INGREDIENTS ———————————— Serves 6

3	ounces chopped pancetta (or 4 ounces chopped bacon)
1/2	bunch quartered broccoli
5	Idaho potatoes
1	cup heavy cream
1	stick butter
	salt to taste
	black pepper to taste

METHOD

1. Preheat oven to 350 degrees. Place the pancetta on a baking sheet and bake till crisp and brown. Set aside, reserving both the pancetta and the drippings.

2. Steam or boil the broccoli for 4 minutes. Remove and set aside.

3. Peel the potatoes and cut into 2-inch pieces. In a large saucepan, cover with water and cook till tender; drain. Remove to a mixing bowl and beat till smooth.

4. Fold in the pancetta, reserved drippings, broccoli, cream and butter. Season with salt and pepper.

SUGAR SNAP PEAS WITH ROASTED PEPPERS AND MUSHROOMS

INGREDIENTS ———————————— Serves 6

2	red Roasted Sweet Peppers (page 71)
1/4	stick butter
3	cups sugar snap peas
2	cups sliced mushrooms
1	teaspoon chopped garlic
1	tablespoon ground horseradish
	salt to taste

METHOD

1. Cut Roasted Sweet Peppers into julienned strips.

2. Melt the butter in a large sauté pan; add the next 4 ingredients. Sauté 5 to 7 minutes or till peas are tender-crisp. Season with salt.

Gluttony is an emotional escape, a sign something is eating us.
—Peter de Vries

1/2 cup = 4 oz • 1 gal = 4 qts = 8 pts = 16 cups = 128 oz • 1 qt = 4 cups = 32 oz • 1 pt = 16 oz = 2 cups

LAZY CHEF NEW POTATOES

12	halved red new potatoes
1	tablespoon chopped garlic
1/4	stick butter
1/4	cup milk
	salt to taste
	black pepper to taste

METHOD

1. In a saucepan, cover the potatoes and garlic with water. Cook till tender; drain.

2. Combine the potatoes with the butter and milk. Mix till smooth; season with salt and pepper.

SMOKED GOUDA MASHED POTATOES

3	medium peeled and chopped Idaho potatoes
1	cup shredded smoked Gouda cheese
1/2	cup milk
2	teaspoons salt
1	teaspoon white pepper

METHOD

1. In a large saucepan, cover the potatoes with water; cook till very tender.

2. In a microwave-safe bowl, combine the cheese and milk. Microwave on high for one minute or till cheese melts; stir to mix well.

3. Drain the potatoes and combine with the cheese mixture in a mixing bowl. Mash till smooth; season with salt and pepper.

How can you govern a country which has 246 varieties of cheese?
—Charles DeGaulle

3 tsp = 1 tbsp • 2 tbsp = 1/8 cup • 4 tbsp = 1/4 cup • 5 tbsp + 1 tsp = 1/3 cup • 1 cup = 8 oz

PAN-FRIED POTATOES

INGREDIENTS ———————————— Serves 6

3	pounds peeled russet potatoes
	salt to taste
1/2	cup butter
1/2	cup canola oil
	black pepper to taste
4	cloves chopped garlic
1/4	cup chopped parsley

METHOD

1. Cut the potatoes into 3/4-inch pieces. Cover with salted water in a saucepan; cook till potatoes are tender but still hold their shape. Drain well.

2. Melt the butter with the oil in a large cast-iron skillet and add the potatoes. Fry without stirring till the potatoes are brown on the bottom. Turn over gently and fry till brown.

3. Season with salt and pepper and spoon into a serving dish. Top with garlic and parsley.

MASHED BONIATO

INGREDIENTS ———————————— Serves 6

2	pounds peeled Boniato potatoes
1	gallon water
1	stick butter
1 1/3	cups milk
1/3	cup sour cream
1	tablespoon salt
1	teaspoon white pepper

METHOD

1. Cut the potatoes into small pieces. Bring the water to a boil in a large saucepan and add potatoes. Cook 45 minutes or till tender; drain completely.

2. Melt the butter with the milk in a small saucepan. Combine with the potatoes, sour cream, salt and pepper in a bowl. Mix with a firm whisk till smooth.

Boniato is a white sweet potato which has become quite popular in Caribbean and Floridian cuisine. The texture is more like a white potato and not quite as sweet as the more familiar sweet potato. People who taste it for the first time are usually delighted.

1/2 cup = 4 oz • 1 gal = 4 qts = 8 pts = 16 cups = 128 oz • 1 qt = 4 cups = 32 oz • 1 pt = 16 oz = 2 cups

OVEN-DRIED TOMATOES

30	Roma tomatoes
	kosher salt
2	cups water
1/2	cup lemon juice
1/4	cup balsamic vinegar
2	tablespoons chopped garlic
2	bay leaves
1	tablespoon oregano
1/2	teaspoon crushed red pepper

METHOD

1. Preheat either a conventional oven to 200 degrees or a convection oven to 175 degrees. Cut tomatoes in half lengthwise and arrange on a baking sheet. Sprinkle with salt. Bake overnight or till dry and firm.

2. Combine rest of ingredients in a saucepan; bring to a boil. Remove from heat and add the tomatoes. Let stand 2 hours to rehydrate.

3. Use in cooking when sun-dried tomatoes are called for or drain and store in olive oil till needed.

CHILE-DUSTED FRIED GREEN TOMATOES WITH FETA CHEESE

1	cup yellow cornmeal
1/2	cup flour
2	tablespoons grated Romano cheese
1	teaspoon crushed red pepper flakes
2	teaspoons salt
5	thickly sliced green tomatoes
3	beaten eggs
1/4	cup melted butter
1/4	cup canola oil
1	cup crumbled feta cheese

METHOD

1. Combine the first 5 ingredients in a bowl; mix well. Dip the tomato slices in the egg and then in the cornmeal mixture. Repeat the process.

2. Heat the butter with the oil in a large sauté pan. Add tomato slices and fry till light brown. Drain on paper towels. Serve topped with feta cheese.

Eating a meal with full awareness can be a powerful, enlightening and healing experience.
—David Simon

3 tsp = 1 tbsp • 2 tbsp = 1/8 cup • 4 tbsp = 1/4 cup • 5 tbsp + 1 tsp = 1/3 cup • 1 cup = 8 oz

CREAMED SPINACH

1/2   cup chopped yellow onion
1   teaspoon chopped garlic
2   tablespoons butter
1   tablespoon flour
1   cup heavy cream
1/4   cup grated Romano cheese
1   cup shredded Monterey Jack cheese
3   cups packed spinach
    salt to taste
    black pepper to taste

METHOD

1. Sauté onion and garlic in butter for 3 minutes. Add flour and stir to mix well.

2. Add the cream and cheeses. Cook over low heat till thickened, stirring constantly. Add the spinach, salt and pepper; mix well. Cook till heated through.

$750 BRAISED ROMAINE

1   tablespoon butter
6   cups coarsely chopped romaine
    salt to taste
    black pepper to taste

METHOD

1. Melt butter in a large sauté pan over medium to high heat. Add romaine.

2. Sauté romaine just till wilted. Season with salt and pepper. Serve immediately.

This expensive recipe had its origins in a sailing trip planned to celebrate my sister Denise's birthday. I was going to cook steaks on my new grill and sauté the vegetables in the galley kitchen. We got off to a late start, and I found myself navigating an unfamiliar waterway in the dark. Sure enough, we hit a sandbar! After a wild attempt to free ourselves, I ended up calling a local towing company which, amazingly, responded in 20 minutes. We were towed to a safe area to anchor overnite. The guy from the towing company handed me a bill for $750! I choked at first, but I paid it. It was 10 o'clock and I still had to cook dinner.

Happy Birthday to Denise, Happy Boating to me...Kaching! Kaching!

1/2 cup = 4 oz • 1 gal = 4 qts = 8 pts = 16 cups = 128 oz • 1 qt = 4 cups = 32 oz • 1 pt = 16 oz = 2 cups

PASTAS & GRAINS

Having grown up in an Irish-Italian household, I remember the aromas of pasta and homemade sauces as they wafted through the house. I have wonderful memories of my mother and grandmothers cooking "from scratch." I used to sit in wonder as they handmade the pasta. In fact, you had to be careful, because in our house, furnishings pulled double duty. I can still hear my grandmothers saying, "Be careful! Can't you see the pasta drying on the bed?"

I remember my mom and my Italian grandmother lovingly stirring the sauces hours on end. All of these homemade dishes were created with affection. No wonder pasta has a special place in my heart; it is an integral part of my natural heritage. When pasta became popular in this country, it was easy for me to create dishes people would enjoy. In this chapter, I share pasta recipes that I learned from my family, as well as traditional Creole recipes that I enjoyed while growing up in Southern Louisiana, working with renowned Chef John Folse.

When preparing a pasta dish, other than rolled or stuffed, I use only high quality imported dry pasta. Whether you're using fresh homemade pasta or dry pasta, cooking time is critical. Thirty seconds can make or break the quality of the pasta's texture.

In addition to pasta, rice is a versatile addition to any meal. Rice is a staple in many cultures. I learned how to appreciate rice growing up on Cajun and Creole cuisine. I spent two years cooking in a Chinese restaurant, so most of my professional experience preparing rice stems from that. Rice works on so many levels because it's easy to prepare. You can cook it with the main dish, or you can prepare it separately and include it after your primary dish has been prepared. In any event, rice adds an interesting bit of taste and texture to many dishes. Like pasta, cooking time is important. I highly recommend adding an automatic rice cooker to your kitchen for simplicity.

LOBSTER MANICOTTI

RICOTTA FILLING
1   pound ricotta cheese
2   eggs
1/2 cup grated Parmesan cheese
2   tablespoons chopped parsley

MANICOTTI SHELLS
6   eggs
1 1/2 cups flour
2   cups milk

SAUCE
1   cup heavy cream
2   cups Marinara Sauce Vignone (page 138)

ASSEMBLY
3   (1 1/2-pound) Maine lobsters
2   tablespoons chopped parsley
1/4 cup finely chopped red bell pepper
1/2 cup thinly shaved Romano cheese

METHOD

1. For the filling, combine all 4 ingredients in a mixing bowl; mix well. Chill in the refrigerator.

2. For the shells, beat the eggs till foamy. Whisk in the flour. Add the milk, whisking till smooth.

3. Preheat an electric skillet to 200 degrees. Ladle 2 tablespoons batter at a time; cook till top is dry. Remove to a paper towel and repeat the process till all the batter is used.

4. Place 2 tablespoons filling in the center of each pasta shell. Fold opposite sides together to meet in the center and overlap slightly.

5. For the sauce, combine the cream and Marinara Sauce Vignone in a saucepan and warm till heated through; do not boil.

6. Boil the lobsters for 12 minutes, remove from shell and keep warm.

7. For the assembly, place the stuffed manicotti on a microwave-safe plate with the warm lobster. Microwave on high for 45 seconds. Top with the prepared sauce and garnish with parsley, bell pepper and Romano cheese.

3 tsp = 1 tbsp • 2 tbsp = 1/8 cup • 4 tbsp = 1/4 cup • 5 tbsp + 1 tsp = 1/3 cup • 1 cup = 8 oz

PREPARING DRIED PASTA

INGREDIENTS ——————— Serves 4

I	gallon water
1/2	pound dried pasta
I	gallon ice water
I	tablespoon canola oil

METHOD

1. Bring water to rapid boil in a large saucepan.

2. Add pasta; cook al dente.

3. Remove from heat and immediately immerse in ice water to stop the cooking process.

4. Drain well and toss with oil.

It is essential to use good quality, imported dried pasta to obtain the al dente texture—the outer surface of the pasta is soft and the center is still firm—which is authentic to Italian pasta dishes. Pasta can be chilled and stored in a Ziplock bag up to 8 hours before using.

PENNE PASTA WITH VODKA SAUCE AND CRAWFISH TAILS

INGREDIENTS ——————— Serves 4

1/2	pound uncooked penne pasta
1 3/4	cups heavy cream
1/2	cup vodka
1/2	cup tomato paste
I	teaspoon chopped garlic
	salt to taste
	black pepper to taste
3/4	cup grated Romano cheese
2	cups (peeled) crawfish tail meat

METHOD

1. For pasta, see Preparing Dried Pasta recipe at left.

2. Combine the next 6 ingredients and 1/2 cup of the cheese in a saucepan; whisk till smooth. Bring to a boil.

3. Add the pasta and crawfish tails to the saucepan. Cook till heated through. Spoon onto serving plates and garnish with remaining cheese.

Everything you see, I owe to spaghetti.
—Sophia Loren

LOBSTER RAVIOLI WITH TRUFFLE AND MUSHROOM SAUCE

LOBSTER FILLING

1 cup cooked and chopped lobster meat	1 tablespoon chopped fresh basil
1 cup ricotta cheese	1 teaspoon chopped garlic
1/4 cup grated Romano cheese	white pepper to taste

RAVIOLI

60 won ton wrappers
cornstarch

SAUCE

1 1/2 cups heavy cream	1 tablespoon truffle oil
1 teaspoon chopped garlic	black pepper to taste
2 tablespoons tomato paste	1/3 cup grated Romano cheese

METHOD

1. For the filling, combine all 6 ingredients in a mixing bowl; mix well. Chill in the refrigerator.

2. For the ravioli, spoon one tablespoon of the lobster mixture onto the center of 30 won ton wrappers. Rub the edge of the wrappers with water and top with the remaining won ton wrappers; press the edges to seal. Dust with cornstarch and chill in the refrigerator.

3. For the sauce, combine the cream, garlic and tomato paste in a saucepan; bring just to a boil. Stir in the oil and pepper. Keep warm.

4. Bring a large saucepan of water to a boil. Add ravioli and cook 2 minutes; drain well. Add to the cream sauce and heat for 30 seconds. Spoon onto serving plates and garnish with cheese.

3 tsp = 1 tbsp • 2 tbsp = 1/8 cup • 4 tbsp = 1/4 cup • 5 tbsp + 1 tsp = 1/3 cup • 1 cup = 8 oz

PENNE PASTA WITH BABY SHRIMP AND MUSHROOM CREAM SAUCE

INGREDIENTS ———————————————————— Serves 4

1/2	pound uncooked penne pasta		2	tablespoons sherry
2	tablespoons butter			salt to taste
2	cups puréed mushrooms			black pepper to taste
1	tablespoon chopped garlic		2	cups peeled (70-90 count) shrimp
2	cups heavy cream		1/2	cup grated Reggiano-Parmigiano cheese

METHOD

1. For pasta, see Preparing Dried Pasta recipe on page 85.

2. Melt the butter in a large sauté pan. Add mushrooms and garlic; sauté for 3 minutes. Add the next 4 ingredients and bring to a boil.

3. Add the shrimp and cook just till pink. Add pasta and toss to coat well with the sauce. Cook till heated through. Spoon onto serving plates and top with cheese.

All food starting with "p" is comfort food: pasta, potato chips, pretzels, peanut butter, pastrami, pizza, pastry.
—Sara Paretsky

1/2 cup = 4 oz • 1 gal = 4 qts = 8 pts = 16 cups = 128 oz • 1 qt = 4 cups = 32 oz • 1 pt = 16 oz = 2 cups

SHEA'S GARLIC LEMON SHRIMP WITH ANGEL HAIR PASTA

1/4	pound uncooked angel hair pasta	1	peeled, seeded and sliced lemon
16	(16-20 count) shrimp		salt to taste
1	stick butter		white pepper to taste
1/4	cup white wine	1/4	cup grated Reggiano-Parmigiano cheese
2	sliced garlic cloves	8	fresh basil leaves

METHOD

1. For pasta, see Preparing Dried Pasta recipe on page 85.

2. Peel and devein the shrimp. Melt the butter in a sauté pan and add the shrimp, wine, garlic and lemon slices. Cook till desired doneness. Season with salt and pepper.

3. Reheat the pasta in the shrimp mixture. Spoon onto serving plates and top with the shrimp mixture. Garnish with cheese and basil.

The most indispensable ingredient of all good home cooking: love for those you are cooking for.
—Sophia Loren

3 tsp = 1 tbsp • 2 tbsp = 1/8 cup • 4 tbsp = 1/4 cup • 5 tbsp + 1 tsp = 1/3 cup • 1 cup = 8 oz

PASTA WITH GRILLED PORK

INGREDIENTS ———————————— Serves 4

I	(8-ounce) can Italian plum tomatoes
I	teaspoon chopped garlic
I	tablespoon chopped fresh basil
2	tablespoons olive oil
1/2	pound uncooked pasta
8	slices pork tenderloin
2	tablespoons Original Chef's Grill Plus
	black pepper to taste
1/2	cup grated Romano cheese

METHOD

1. Combine the first 4 ingredients in a large saucepan and cook over high heat for 3 minutes. Reduce heat and simmer 5 minutes longer.

2. For pasta, see Preparing Dried Pasta recipe on page 85.

3. Preheat grill to high heat. Brush the pork tenderloin with the Chef's Grill Plus. Grill the pork just till cooked through. Toss pasta and pork with heated tomato sauce. Season with pepper.

4. Spoon onto serving plates and garnish with cheese. Serve immediately.

The grilled pork can be replaced with peeled and deveined shrimp, boneless chicken breasts or beef tenderloin if preferred.

DUCK AND SHIITAKE MUSHROOM PASTA

INGREDIENTS ———————————— Serves 8

I	pound uncooked linguine
I	tablespoon canola oil
3	cups roasted sliced duck meat
3	cups sliced shiitake mushrooms
I	teaspoon chopped garlic
1/2	cup chopped green onions
I	cup Duck Stock (page 131)
	black pepper to taste
1 1/2	cups chopped Brie cheese
1/2	cup grated Romano cheese

METHOD

1. For pasta, see Preparing Dried Pasta recipe on page 85.

2. Heat the oil in a sauté pan on medium heat. Add the next 6 ingredients; bring to a boil.

3. Add the pasta and cook till heated through. Spoon onto serving plates and garnish with cheese.

THREE CHEESE MACARONI

INGREDIENTS ——————— Serves 4

1/2	pound uncooked elbow macaroni
1	cup shredded white Cheddar cheese
1/4	cup grated Romano cheese
1/2	cup crumbled blue cheese
1 1/4	cups heavy cream
1	egg
	black pepper to taste
1/2	cup fine bread crumbs

METHOD

1. Preheat oven to 350 degrees. Cook the pasta using the package directions and drain.

2. Combine 1/2 cup Cheddar and next 5 ingredients in a bowl; mix well. Add the pasta. Spoon into a small baking dish.

3. Bake 10 minutes. Let stand at room temperature 20 minutes. Sprinkle with bread crumbs and remaining Cheddar. Bake 5 minutes longer or till bread crumbs are golden brown and cheese melts.

CAJUN PORK AND CHICKEN JAMBALAYA

INGREDIENTS ——————— Serves 4

1	large boneless skinless chicken breast
4	teaspoons Habanero Chef's Grill Plus
1 1/2	cups water
1/2	(10-ounce) can cream of mushroom soup
1/2	cup chopped green onions
1 1/2	cups uncooked instant rice
1/2	finely chopped smoked link sausage
	salt to taste

METHOD

1. Preheat grill to high heat. Brush the chicken with 2 teaspoons Chef's Grill Plus. Grill till cooked through.

2. Combine the water, soup and onions in a saucepan and bring to a boil. Add the rice and sausage. Simmer 10 minutes. Chop the chicken and add to rice mixture with 2 teaspoons Chef's Grill Plus. Cook till heated through. Season with salt and serve immediately.

*You have to try Chef's Grill Plus®.
I can't tell you the number of people who call or write and say they can't live without it. Your food will taste better, look more appealing and you'll be healthier because of it.
—Chef Tim Creehan, Inventor*

3 tsp = 1 tbsp • 2 tbsp = 1/8 cup • 4 tbsp = 1/4 cup • 5 tbsp + 1 tsp = 1/3 cup • 1 cup = 8 oz

VEGETABLE RISOTTO

SAFFRON RICE

VEGETABLE RISOTTO

INGREDIENTS ———————————— Serves 8

1/4   cup canola oil
1 1/4 cups uncooked super fino arborio rice
3 1/2 cups water or Chicken Stock (page 130)
1/2   cup chopped tomatoes
1   teaspoon chopped garlic
1   cup red wine
1 1/4 cups heavy cream
1/2   cup chopped zucchini
1/2   cup chopped mushrooms
1/4   cup grated Romano cheese
2   teaspoons salt
1/2   teaspoon white pepper

METHOD

1. Heat the oil in a large sauté pan. Add
    the rice and sauté lightly. Add the water,
    tomatoes and garlic; mix well.

2. Stir in the remaining ingredients. Cook
    till heated through. Serve with additional
    grated cheese.

SAFFRON RICE

INGREDIENTS ———————————— Serves 4

1   tablespoon olive oil
1   cup uncooked basmati rice
1/2   chopped yellow onion
1   cup chopped green onions
1   teaspoon chopped garlic
1   gram saffron
2   cups Chicken Stock (page 130)
       pinch of salt
1   teaspoon black pepper

METHOD

1. Heat the oil in a sauté pan and add the
    next 5 ingredients. Sauté for 5 minutes.

2. Stir in the Chicken Stock and season
    with salt and pepper. Bring to a boil and
    reduce the heat. Simmer, covered, for
    18 minutes.

*With coarse rice to eat, with
water to drink, and my bended
arm for a pillow—I still have joy in
the midst of these things.
—Confucius*

1/2 cup = 4 oz • 1 gal = 4 qts = 8 pts = 16 cups = 128 oz • 1 qt = 4 cups = 32 oz • 1 pt = 16 oz = 2 cups

MOCK RISOTTO WITH ASPARAGUS AND SHIITAKES

4   cups cooked rice
2   cups heavy cream
1   cup grated Reggiano-Parmigiano cheese
1   cup sliced shiitake mushrooms
1   teaspoon chopped garlic
1   cup cooked and chilled asparagus
    salt to taste
    black pepper to taste

METHOD

1. Combine the rice with the cream in a saucepan and cook till heated through, stirring frequently. Add cheese, mushrooms and garlic; mix gently. Simmer over low heat for 5 minutes.

2. Chop the asparagus; add and simmer till heated through. Season with salt and pepper and spoon into a serving bowl.

PORCINI RISOTTO

INGREDIENTS ———————————— Serves 4

1   tablespoon canola oil
1   cup uncooked super fino arborio rice
1   teaspoon chopped garlic
6   cups water
1 1/2 tablespoons porcini powder
      pinch of crushed red pepper
1/2   teaspoon fresh thyme leaves
2   tablespoons heavy cream

METHOD

1. Heat the oil in a large sauté pan. Add the rice and garlic; fry briefly. Add water gradually while stirring constantly and adding the porcini powder.

2. Bring to a boil and reduce to a simmer, stirring constantly. Cook 20 minutes, or till thick, stirring constantly. Remove from heat and stir in the pepper, thyme and cream.

Tell me what you eat, and I will tell you what you are.
—Anthelme Brillat-Savarin

3 tsp = 1 tbsp • 2 tbsp = 1/8 cup • 4 tbsp = 1/4 cup • 5 tbsp + 1 tsp = 1/3 cup • 1 cup = 8 oz

SOFT CHEESE POLENTA WITH TOMATO SAUCE

INGREDIENTS ———————————— Serves 8

1 1/2 cups canned Italian plum tomatoes
1   teaspoon chopped garlic
2   tablespoons chopped fresh basil
1   tablespoon olive oil
       salt to taste
       black pepper to taste
1   (7-ounce) bag polenta
2   cups shredded Fontina cheese
       grated Romano cheese to taste
       heavy cream

METHOD

1. Combine the first 6 ingredients in a food processor. Process till the tomatoes are coarsely chopped. Let stand in a warm place.

2. For polenta, follow package cooking instructions. Add cheese, stirring to melt and mix well. Add cream to desired consistency. Spoon onto serving plates and top with the tomato mixture.

CHEESE GRITS

INGREDIENTS ———————————— Serves 12

6   cups water
1 1/2 cups uncooked white grits
1/2   cup heavy cream
1/4   cup shredded white Cheddar cheese
       salt to taste
       white pepper to taste

METHOD

1. Bring the water to a boil in a large saucepan and stir in the grits. Cook for 45 minutes to one hour or till soft, stirring frequently.

2. Add cream and cheese; mix well. Season with salt and pepper.

Yeah, I want my cheesy poofs.
—Eric Cartman, Southpark

1/2 cup = 4 oz • 1 gal = 4 qts = 8 pts = 16 cups = 128 oz • 1 qt = 4 cups = 32 oz • 1 pt = 16 oz = 2 cups

MEATS

Food trends come and go. After a brief period of complicated cuisine, many of the classics and comfort foods have re-emerged as standards in American cuisine. That's why a great steak will always be considered one of life's finest pleasures. Most everyone enjoys a prime, perfectly aged steak, charbroiled and sizzling in its own natural juices. Believe it or not, there are a few secrets to cooking a great steak. Once you apply the following technical information, cooking meat will become one of your most satisfying experiences.

A friend of mine, Dennis Stiffler, Ph.D., is a world-famous expert on beef. Dennis has worked with many of the premier steak houses and meat purveyors. His favorite purveyor of beef is Allen Brothers of Chicago, which happens to be one of mine as well. When it comes to choosing the perfect steak, Dennis doesn't mince words:

"In today's world of consolidation, mass production, and beef as a commodity product, you should never settle for an unacceptable product. In fact, you should *demand* a great product from your supplier. Doing the job right requires extra time and effort. Hand-selecting, sorting, sizing, documenting the aging, choosing the finest craftsmen to portion the product—all work together to ensure product performance, presentation on the plate and unsurpassed eating satisfaction. I call this *sciencing* the product.

"Choosing a cut of beef that has been properly aged is the secret to selecting the perfect steak. I recommend that you identify the aging time as four-to-five weeks for boneless cuts and four weeks for bone-in cuts. If you are roasting and grilling, allow the cut to rest 10-15 minutes at room temperature after it has been cooked. Resting allows the cut to re-absorb some of the moisture and relaxes muscle fibers tightened during grilling.

"Aging dramatically improves beef tenderness, provides distinct texture, and imparts unique flavor characteristics. Cooked beef flavor is determined, for the most part, by fat—both marbling and surface fat. The flavor of aged beef is the result of the interaction between the components of fat and the ripening of the meat.

"You don't have to be a rocket scientist to choose the right cut of beef, but it can be quite scientific. The longer beef is aged, the more the muscle proteins break down ensuring product performance; however, maximum tenderness and the progress of tenderization during aging varies among certain cuts of beef. Tenderloin requires less aging than strip loins, rib eyes or short loins. Top sirloin butts require a longer period of aging than do other middle meats.

"There are two forms of aging: wet-aged, in a bag, or dry-aged, aged 'naked.' Research on the subject suggests there is little or no difference in the tenderness of wet-aged beef and dry-aged beef. Wet-aged beef is sealed in a vacuum-packaged bag to protect the meat from the air, prevent moisture loss and control certain microbial growth. Steaks from wet-aged beef are generally considered to be juicier than steaks from dry-aged beef.

"Dry-aged beef is exposed to the air under controlled conditions—time, temperature, humidity and sometimes ultra-violet light—to effectively manage the moisture loss during aging and certain microorganisms. Significant moisture loss concentrates certain flavor components, such as fat and proteins, which enhance the taste and heighten the flavor. The unique flavors are often described as 'nutty, buttery, or earthy.'"

Now that you have heard from Dr. Stiffler, instead of preparing your steak with all types of rubs and spices, take the time to choose the perfect cut of beef, make sure it has been aged properly, then prepare it simply. You're ready to open a nice bottle of red wine and enjoy one of the world's great classics.

And speaking of the classics, after dazzling the crowd at a local Alzheimer's Benefit, Steve Cropper, a member of the Blues Brothers Band and the Rock and Roll Hall of Fame, visited my restaurant. Cropper, you may recall, co-wrote the lyrics for *Sittin' on the Dock of the Bay* and *In the Midnight Hour*. When he finished his dinner, Cropper left me this inscription on the label of his wine bottle: "Best dang steak I ever had."

CRISP BONELESS DUCK

2	(4 to 5-pound) Long Island ducks	3	cups Duck Stock (page 131)
1/4	cup soy sauce	1/2	recipe Mashed Boniato (page 79)
	granulated garlic to taste	1	recipe Sautéed Baby Green Beans (page 73)
	salt to taste	4	baked puff pastry crescents
	black pepper to taste	4	fresh rosemary sprigs
1	cup Madeira wine		

METHOD

1. Preheat oven to 400 degrees. Brush the ducks with the soy sauce and season generously with garlic, salt and pepper. Place on a rack in a roasting pan and roast for 1 1/2 hours or till the skin is brown and the legs move freely. Let stand till cool. Split ducks lengthwise and place skin side down on a work surface. Remove the back, rib and breast bones. Cut the skin on the wing and leg bones and carefully pull the bones out from the inside.

2. Increase oven temperature to 500 degrees. Place the ducks skin side up on the rack in the roasting pan. Roast 15 minutes or till the skin is crisp. Remove ducks from the pan, reserving pan drippings. Place the roasting pan over high heat on the stove top; add wine and Duck Stock. Cook till reduced to desired consistency. Spoon the Mashed Boniato onto serving plates. Top with duck and spoon reduced sauce over the top. Garnish with Sautéed Baby Green Beans, a puff pastry crescent and a rosemary sprig.

For Raspberry Duck, add 1/2 cup raspberry purée to the sauce procedure and sugar to taste.

A GREAT STEAK

2   tablespoons granulated garlic
2   tablespoons kosher salt
2   tablespoons freshly ground black pepper
4   (favorite cut) steaks at room temperature

METHOD

1. Preheat a grill surface till very hot. Combine garlic, salt and pepper in a small bowl. Sprinkle generously over both sides of the steaks.

2. Place the steaks on the grill surface. Grill till bottom side is browned and charred. Turn and cook to desired doneness. Let rest for 5 minutes; serve.

Best dang steak I ever had.
—Steve Cropper

FILET MY WAY

4   (6-ounce) tenderloin filets at room temperature
       granulated garlic to taste
       salt to taste
       black pepper to taste
1/2   stick butter

METHOD

1. Season the filets on both sides with garlic, salt and pepper.

2. Heat the butter in a large sauté pan and add the steaks. Sear on both sides and cook to desired doneness. Top with browned butter.

Sacred cows make the best hamburger.
—Mark Twain

3 tsp = 1 tbsp • 2 tbsp = 1/8 cup • 4 tbsp = 1/4 cup • 5 tbsp + 1 tsp = 1/3 cup • 1 cup = 8 oz

FILETS WITH CRAB MEAT, HOLLANDAISE AND A
BLACK PEPPER BUTTER SAUCE

INGREDIENTS ——————————————————————————— Serves 4

FILETS

4	(6-ounce) choice tenderloin steaks at room temperature	kosher salt to taste
	granulated garlic to taste	black pepper to taste
		1 recipe Hollandaise Sauce (page 154)

BLACK PEPPER BUTTER SAUCE

1/2	cup Worcestershire sauce	1 tablespoon black pepper
1	tablespoon lemon juice	1/2 cup heavy cream
1	teaspoon chopped garlic	1 stick butter, chopped

SAUTÉED LUMP CRAB MEAT

1/4	stick butter	salt to taste
1/2	pound jumbo lump crab meat	white pepper to taste
1	chopped green onion	1 recipe Lazy Chef New Potatoes (page 78)
2	teaspoons lemon juice	

METHOD

1. For the steaks, preheat a grill surface. Season steaks with garlic, salt and pepper; grill to desired doneness.

2. For the sauce, while the steaks are cooking, combine the first 4 ingredients in a small saucepan; cook till reduced by half. Add cream and reduce to sauce consistency. Whisk butter in gradually. Set aside; keep warm.

3. For the crab, melt butter in a sauté pan. Add the next 3 ingredients; season with salt and pepper. Heat thoroughly.

4. When the steaks are done, remove and let rest for 5 minutes. Serve steaks over Lazy Chef New Potatoes and drizzle the Black Pepper Butter Sauce over the steaks. Top with Sautéed Lump Crab Meat and Hollandaise Sauce.

1/2 cup = 4 oz • 1 gal = 4 qts = 8 pts = 16 cups = 128 oz • 1 qt = 4 cups = 32 oz • 1 pt = 16 oz = 2 cups

CHIMICHURRI STEAK

INGREDIENTS ———————————— Serves 8

CHIMICHURRI SAUCE

1	cup extra-virgin olive oil
2	tablespoons lemon juice
2	tablespoons chopped garlic
1	bunch parsley
1	tablespoon kosher salt
1	tablespoon crushed red pepper flakes

STEAKS

4	(14-ounce) ribeye steaks at room temperature
	granulated garlic to taste
	kosher salt to taste
	black pepper to taste
1	recipe Roasted Garlic (page 72)
1/4	cup chopped parsley

METHOD

1. For the sauce, combine all 6 ingredients in a food processor; process until smooth. Spoon into a bowl and let stand one hour.

2. For the steaks, preheat a grill surface. Season the steaks with garlic, salt and pepper. Grill to desired doneness. Let rest for 5 minutes. Place on a cutting board and cut diagonally into thin slices. Serve topped with sauce. Garnish with Roasted Garlic and parsley.

RIBEYE WITH MOREL MUSHROOMS AND MAYTAG BLUE CHEESE

INGREDIENTS ———————————— Serves 4

1/4	cup dried morel mushrooms
1/4	cup brandy
1/3	cup Veal Glace (page 134)
1	cup heavy cream
1/4	cup Maytag blue cheese
	ground black pepper to taste
2	thick-cut ribeye steaks at room temperature
2	tablespoons Original Chef's Grill Plus
1	tablespoon chopped parsley

METHOD

1. Soak the mushrooms in brandy in a bowl overnight. Pour into a saucepan and heat on high; flambé. After the flames subside add Veal Glace, cream and blue cheese. Cook till reduced to a thick consistency. Season with pepper.

2. Preheat a grill surface to high. Brush the steaks with the Chef's Grill Plus. Grill to desired doneness.

3. Remove the steaks and let rest for 5 minutes. Slice across grain and place on serving plates. Top with mushroom sauce and parsley.

3 tsp = 1 tbsp • 2 tbsp = 1/8 cup • 4 tbsp = 1/4 cup • 5 tbsp + 1 tsp = 1/3 cup • 1 cup = 8 oz

BLUE CHEESE STEAK

2	cups soy sauce		1	tablespoon ground black pepper
1	tablespoon rice vinegar		1	whole flank steak
1	tablespoon chopped garlic		1	cup crumbled blue cheese

METHOD

1. Combine the first 4 ingredients in a shallow dish; mix well. Add the steak. Marinate overnight; drain.

2. Preheat a grill surface. Grill steak over high heat to desired doneness. Remove to a cutting board; let stand for 5 minutes.

3. Slice the steak diagonally across the grain. Serve topped with blue cheese.

Flank steak is a very inexpensive cut that can really shine when properly prepared. This dish is great to serve with fresh bread as a sandwich or over steamed rice.

1/2 cup = 4 oz • 1 gal = 4 qts = 8 pts = 16 cups = 128 oz • 1 qt = 4 cups = 32 oz • 1 pt = 16 oz = 2 cups

FLANK STEAKS WITH SHALLOT BUTTER

INGREDIENTS ———————————— Serves 4

4	(6-ounce) flank steaks at room temperature
	kosher salt to taste
	freshly ground black pepper to taste
2	tablespoons canola oil
1	stick butter
4	sliced shallots
2	teaspoons chopped garlic
2	tablespoons red wine vinegar
1	cup red wine
1/2	cup Veal Stock (page 134)
2	tablespoons chopped parsley

METHOD

1. Preheat oven to 225 degrees. Season the steaks on both sides with salt and pepper. Preheat a cast-iron skillet and add the oil. Sear steaks on both sides. Remove to an oven-safe platter and keep warm in the oven.

2. Place one tablespoon of butter in the cast-iron skillet used to sear the steak. Add shallots and garlic and sauté for 5 minutes; do not brown. Add the vinegar and cook till it evaporates. Add the wine and Veal Stock; cook till the liquid is reduced by half. Remove from heat and add remaining butter, swirling till the butter melts.

3. Slice the steaks diagonally. Place on serving plates and top with sauce and parsley. Serve with roasted potatoes.

SIRLOIN STEAKS WITH OYSTER MUSHROOM SAUCE

INGREDIENTS ———————————— Serves 4

OYSTER MUSHROOM SAUCE

1/2	cup red wine
1	cup Veal Glace (page 134)
1	teaspoon chopped garlic
1/2	pound oyster mushrooms
1	stick butter
	salt to taste
	black pepper to taste

STEAKS

| 4 | (6-ounce) sirloin steaks at room temperature |
| 3 | tablespoons Original Chef's Grill Plus |

METHOD

1. For the sauce, combine the first 4 ingredients in a medium saucepan; cook till reduced to sauce consistency. Whisk in butter gradually. Season with salt and pepper.

2. For the steaks, preheat a grill surface on high. Apply Chef's Grill Plus using package directions. Grill to desired doneness.

3. Place on serving plates and drizzle with sauce.

Don't take a butcher's advice on how to cook meat. If he knew, he'd be a chef.
—Andy Rooney

3 tsp = 1 tbsp • 2 tbsp = 1/8 cup • 4 tbsp = 1/4 cup • 5 tbsp + 1 tsp = 1/3 cup • 1 cup = 8 oz

BLACK PEPPER CRUSTED SIRLOIN WITH A PINEAPPLE TWIST

1/2	cup cracked black pepper
4	(12-ounce) New York strip steaks at room temperature
	salt to taste
1/4	stick butter
1/4	cup brandy
1/2	cup Veal Stock (page 134)
1/2	cup heavy cream
1/4	cup chopped pineapple
1/4	cup chopped green onions

METHOD

1. Press the pepper onto the steaks and season with salt. Heat the butter in a large sauté pan; sear steaks well on both sides. Remove from the sauté pan to an oven-safe platter. If necessary, roast at 400 degrees to desired doneness.

2. Add the brandy to the sauté pan. Flambé and allow the flames to subside. Add the Veal Stock, cream and pineapple. Cook till reduced to desired consistency.

3. Place steaks on serving plates. Top with sauce and onions.

Steak au Poivre is a classical dish which, when executed correctly, is always wonderful. Through experimentation I have found that the pineapple adds a unique dimension.

BISTECCA

1/4	cup julienned onion
1	tablespoon chopped garlic
1/4	cup olive oil
1	tablespoon lemon juice
1	teaspoon chopped rosemary
	kosher salt to taste
	black pepper to taste
4	(12-ounce) strip steaks at room temperature

METHOD

1. Sauté onion and garlic in the oil in a sauté pan just till tender. Combine with the next 4 ingredients in a shallow dish; mix well. Trim the steaks and add to the marinade. Marinate at room temperature for 3 hours; drain.

2. Preheat a grill surface and grill the steaks to desired doneness. Remove to a cutting board and slice diagonally across the grain.

Bistecca—known in the English-speaking world as a Porterhouse steak—steak containing a single bone, attached to the sirloin strip and filet. We simplify by using the strip steak only.

1/2 cup = 4 oz • 1 gal = 4 qts = 8 pts = 16 cups = 128 oz • 1 qt = 4 cups = 32 oz • 1 pt = 16 oz = 2 cups

BEEF TIPS TARRAGON

2	tablespoons melted butter	1	coarsely chopped green bell pepper
1	teaspoon coarsely chopped garlic	1	cup quartered mushrooms
1	teaspoon dried tarragon leaves	3	tablespoons brandy
1	teaspoon cracked black pepper	1/3	cup Veal Glace (page 134)
20	(1 to 2-ounce) beef filet tips	1	cup heavy cream
1	coarsely chopped yellow onion		salt to taste

METHOD

1. Heat butter in a sauté pan and add the garlic, tarragon and black pepper; sauté lightly. Add the filet tips and cook to desired doneness. Remove beef to a bowl with a slotted spoon.

2. Add onion, green pepper and mushrooms to the saucepan; sauté briefly over high heat. Stir in the brandy. Flambé and allow the flames to subside. Stir in the Veal Glace and cream; season with salt. Cook till thickened, stirring frequently.

3. Return filet tips to sauté pan and cook till heated through.

Beef tip recipes are a great way to use meat trimmings. The sauce in this recipe is similar to the one in the Black Pepper-Crusted Sirloin on page 103, but the addition of the onions, green peppers and mushrooms creates quite a different dish.

3 tsp = 1 tbsp • 2 tbsp = 1/8 cup • 4 tbsp = 1/4 cup • 5 tbsp + 1 tsp = 1/3 cup • 1 cup = 8 oz

RIBEYE ROAST STUFFED WITH GARLIC AND ROSEMARY

INGREDIENTS ———————————— Serves 8

1/2 cup extra-virgin olive oil
1/4 cup chopped garlic
1/2 cup chopped fresh rosemary
1/4 cup black pepper
1   (4 to 5-pound) whole ribeye at
     room temperature
     kosher salt to taste

METHOD

1. Preheat oven to 450 degrees. Combine the first 4 ingredients in a blender or food processor; process till smooth.

2. Cut the meat open by cutting along the spiral fat line into the ribeye. When cutting the ribeye, picture unrolling the roast like a piece of carpet, leaving one flat piece to be rolled back up. Brush the oil mixture on the cut sides of the roast and close the roast; secure with kitchen twine. Season with salt.

3. Place on a rack in a roasting pan and insert a meat thermometer. Roast to desired doneness. Let stand for several minutes before carving.

120–125 degrees: rare
125–135 degrees: medium-rare
135–140 degrees: medium
145 degrees: thoroughly cooked

LAMB CHOPS DIJONNAISE

INGREDIENTS ———————————— Serves 2

1   rack of lamb at room temperature
     kosher salt to taste
     black pepper to taste
2   tablespoons white wine
1   tablespoon lemon juice
1/4 cup Veal Stock (page 134)
1/4 cup heavy cream
1/4 cup Dijon mustard
1   teaspoon chopped garlic

METHOD

1. Season the lamb generously with salt and pepper. Grill to desired doneness.

2. Combine the remaining ingredients in a medium saucepan; mix well. Cook till reduced by half.

3. Cut lamb into chops and serve with the mustard sauce.

A gourmet is just a glutton with brains.
—Philip W. Haberman, Vogue,
January 1961

ASIAN MARINATED LAMB CHOPS

1/2	cup soy sauce	1	tablespoon chopped pickled ginger
1/4	cup rice vinegar	1	tablespoon chopped garlic
1	cup canola oil	1	teaspoon chopped fresh mint
2	teaspoons Thai chile sauce	16	lamb chops
	juice and halves of an orange		

METHOD

1. Combine the first 8 ingredients in a shallow dish; mix well. Add the lamb chops and marinate at room temperature for 2 hours minimum; drain.

2. Preheat grill surface to high. Add lamb chops and grill to desired doneness. Serve immediately.

You may reserve the marinade and bring it to a boil to use as a sauce for the lamb chops. I highly recommend a sealed marinating container so the lamb can be rotated frequently.

3 tsp = 1 tbsp • 2 tbsp = 1/8 cup • 4 tbsp = 1/4 cup • 5 tbsp + 1 tsp = 1/3 cup • 1 cup = 8 oz

RACK OF LAMB WITH ROASTED VEGETABLES

INGREDIENTS ———————————————————————— Serves 2

I	(2 to 2¹/2-pound) 8-bone rack of domestic lamb	I	coarsely chopped zucchini
	granulated garlic to taste	¹/2	julienned yellow onion
	kosher salt to taste	I	cup quartered mushrooms
	cracked pepper to taste	¹/2	cup red wine
I	coarsely chopped carrot	¹/4	cup Veal Glace (page 134)
I	coarsely chopped yellow squash	I	fresh rosemary sprig
		¹/4	stick butter, chopped

METHOD

1. Preheat oven to 450 degrees. Season the lamb generously on all sides with garlic, salt and pepper. Place on a rack in an ovenproof sauté pan and arrange the carrot, squash, zucchini, onion and mushrooms around the rack. Roast for 20 minutes or to desired doneness. Remove the lamb and vegetables to a plate. If rare to medium-rare is desired, remove rack but allow vegetables to fully cook before removing.

2. Place the sauté pan on the stove top and add the wine, Veal Glace and rosemary, stirring to de-glaze the pan. Cook till sauce is reduced to a thick consistency. Add butter gradually, whisking till smooth after each addition.

3. Place lamb on a cutting board and cut into chops. Serve with the vegetables and spoon sauce over the top.

If you throw a lamb chop in the oven, what's to keep it from getting done?
—Joan Crawford

¹/2 cup = 4 oz • I gal = 4 qts = 8 pts = I6 cups = I28 oz • I qt = 4 cups = 32 oz • I pt = I6 oz = 2 cups

PORK RIB CHOPS WITH MOREL MUSHROOM SAUCE

MOREL MUSHROOM SAUCE

1/4 cup dried morel mushrooms	pinch of chopped garlic
1/4 cup brandy	salt to taste
1/2 cup Veal Stock (page 134)	white pepper to taste
1 1/2 cups heavy cream	

PORK

4 (12-ounce) rib chops	1/2 cup flour
kosher salt to taste	1/4 cup melted butter
white pepper to taste	

METHOD

1. For the sauce, combine the mushrooms with the brandy in a small bowl and let soak for one hour or longer. Transfer to a sauté pan and heat the mixture. Flambé and allow the flames to subside. Add the Veal Stock, cream and garlic; mix well. Cook till reduced and thickened to desired consistency. Season with salt and pepper. Keep warm.

2. For the pork, preheat oven to 450 degrees. Season pork with salt and pepper; dust with flour. Heat butter in an ovenproof sauté pan and add the pork. Sear evenly on both sides. Place sauté pan in the oven and roast for 15 to 20 minutes or to desired doneness.

3. Remove the chops; let rest for 5 minutes. Top with sauce.

> *I hate people who are not serious*
> *about their meals.*
> *—Oscar Wilde*

VEAL STEAK

4	(8-ounce) veal steaks		1/4	cup melted butter
	salt to taste		1/2	cup Veal Glace (page 134)
	white pepper to taste		1/2	cup Meunière Sauce (page 154)
1	cup flour		12	steamed asparagus stalks

METHOD

1. Preheat oven to 400 degrees. Season the veal with salt and pepper and dust with flour. Heat butter in an ovenproof sauté pan till very hot. Add veal and sauté 30 seconds on each side or till light brown. Place sauté pan in the oven and roast to desired doneness.

2. Spoon 2 tablespoons of the Veal Glace on one side of each serving plate and 2 tablespoons of the Meunière Sauce on the other side. Place one veal steak in the center of each plate. Serve topped with asparagus.

Eating well gives a spectacular joy to life.
—Elsa Schiaparelli, Shocking Life

1/2 cup = 4 oz • 1 gal = 4 qts = 8 pts = 16 cups = 128 oz • 1 qt = 4 cups = 32 oz • 1 pt = 16 oz = 2 cups

VENISON STEAK WITH TOMATO BASIL BUTTER SAUCE

4	(8-ounce) venison strip loin steaks
	kosher salt to taste
	white pepper to taste
1/2	cup flour
2	tablespoons canola oil
1/2	cup chopped tomato
2	teaspoons chopped garlic

1/2	cup red wine
1/4	cup Veal Glace (page 134)
1/2	stick butter, chopped
2	tablespoons chopped fresh basil
1	recipe Sweet Potato Mash (page 74)
1	recipe Tobacco Onions (page 72)

METHOD

1. Preheat oven to 400 degrees. Season the steaks with salt and pepper. Dust in flour. Heat the oil in a sauté pan till almost smoking. Add venison and sear on both sides. Place in the oven for 10 to 12 minutes or to desired doneness.

2. Remove the steaks from pan and keep warm. In the same pan, add tomato and garlic; sauté lightly. Add the wine and Veal Glace; cook until reduced by half. Whisk in butter gradually until fully incorporated. Stir in basil.

3. Place steaks on Sweet Potato Mash. Top with sauce and Tobacco Onions.

Vegetables are interesting but lack a sense of purpose when unaccompanied by a good cut of meat.
—Fran Lebowitz

3 tsp = 1 tbsp • 2 tbsp = 1/8 cup • 4 tbsp = 1/4 cup • 5 tbsp + 1 tsp = 1/3 cup • 1 cup = 8 oz

TUSCAN-STYLE ROASTED CHICKEN

INGREDIENTS ——————————————————— Serves 4

1	whole chicken	5	pitted and halved kalamata olives
4	quartered new potatoes	2	sprigs fresh rosemary
1	peeled and sliced large carrot	1	pound sliced Italian sausage
6	quartered mushrooms		kosher salt to taste
1	chopped yellow onion		black pepper to taste
1	chopped zucchini	2	cups Chicken Stock (page 130)
5	whole garlic cloves		

METHOD

1. Preheat oven to 350 degrees. Cut chicken into 8 pieces. Place the next 9 ingredients in a large roasting pan. Season the chicken with salt and pepper; arrange skin side up over the vegetables. Roast till the juices run clear. If a crispier skin texture is desired, turn broiler to high and broil till desired texture.

2. Place roasting pan on the stove top. Add Chicken Stock and reduce to desired consistency. Remove the chicken and vegetable mixture to a serving platter; top with the sauce.

One cannot think well, love well, sleep well, if one has not dined well.
—*Virginia Woolf*, A Room of One's Own

PAN-SAUTÉED CHICKEN WITH LEMON-CAPER SAUCE

INGREDIENTS ———————— Serves 4

1	cup bread crumbs
1/4	cup grated Romano cheese
1	teaspoon black pepper
2	tablespoons Original Chef's Grill Plus
1/4	cup milk
4	(6-ounce) boneless skinless chicken breasts
1/2	stick butter
1	teaspoon chopped garlic
1	tablespoon capers
1/4	cup white wine
1	tablespoon lemon juice
1/2	stick butter, chopped
1	tablespoon chopped parsley

METHOD

1. Preheat oven to 450 degrees. Mix bread crumbs, cheese and pepper in a bowl. Whisk the Chef's Grill Plus with the milk in a bowl. Dip the chicken into Chef's Grill Plus mixture, and then press it into the bread crumb mixture, coating evenly.

2. Melt 1/2 stick butter in a large sauté pan. Add chicken and sauté till brown on both sides. Remove to an oven-safe platter and bake 10 minutes.

3. Add garlic, capers, wine and lemon juice to the sauté pan and cook till reduced to desired consistency. Whisk in 1/2 stick butter gradually and stir in parsley. Serve over chicken.

GRILLED CHICKEN WITH SPICY BASIL CREAM SAUCE

INGREDIENTS ———————— Serves 4

1/2	cup Chicken Stock (page 130)
3/4	cup heavy cream
3	teaspoons lemon juice
1/2	cup finely chopped basil
1	tablespoon chopped garlic
1	teaspoon kosher salt
1	teaspoon crushed red pepper
4	(6-ounce) boneless skinless chicken breasts
4	tablespoons Original Chef's Grill Plus
2	tablespoons chopped Roasted Sweet Peppers (page 71)

METHOD

1. Combine first 7 ingredients in a saucepan; mix well. Cook over medium heat till thickened to sauce consistency. Keep warm over low heat.

2. Preheat a grill surface. Brush the chicken with Chef's Grill Plus. Grill till cooked through.

3. Top with sauce and Roasted Sweet Peppers.

Anyone can hold the helm when the sea is calm.
—Publilius Syrus

3 tsp = 1 tbsp • 2 tbsp = 1/8 cup • 4 tbsp = 1/4 cup • 5 tbsp + 1 tsp = 1/3 cup • 1 cup = 8 oz

KUNG PAO CHICKEN

MARINADE

1	tablespoon canola oil		salt to taste
2	egg whites		white pepper to taste
1/4	cup cornstarch		

CHICKEN AND VEGETABLES

2	cups chopped chicken leg meat	1/4	cup sliced carrot
1	cup chopped yellow onion	1/2	cup shelled peanuts
1/2	cup chopped green bell pepper	1/4	cup canola oil
1/4	cup chopped bamboo shoots		dried Szechuan chiles to taste

STIR-FRY SAUCE

1/2	cup soy sauce	1	tablespoon sugar
1/2	cup Chicken Stock (page 130)	1	teaspoon chopped garlic
2	tablespoons rice vinegar	1	teaspoon chopped gingerroot
1	tablespoon dry sherry	1	teaspoon black pepper

METHOD

1. For the marinade, combine all 5 ingredients in a bowl; whisk till smooth.

2. For the chicken and vegetables, combine marinade with chicken and let stand 30 minutes. Mix the next 5 ingredients in a bowl. Heat a wok and add 1/4 cup oil. Add chicken mixture and vegetables; stir-fry till chicken is cooked through. Remove to a bowl. Add the dried chiles to the wok; stir-fry till blackened.

3. For the stir-fry sauce, combine all 8 ingredients; mix well. Add to wok. Cook till slightly reduced. Return chicken and vegetables; cook till heated through. Serve with steamed rice.

1/2 cup = 4 oz • 1 gal = 4 qts = 8 pts = 16 cups = 128 oz • 1 qt = 4 cups = 32 oz • 1 pt = 16 oz = 2 cups

BONELESS QUAIL STUFFED WITH SHIITAKE MUSHROOMS AND RICE

INGREDIENTS ———————————————————————— Serves 6

SHIITAKE MUSHROOM AND RICE STUFFING

1/2 cup chopped Andouille sausage	1/2 cup chopped green onions
1 cup sliced shiitake mushrooms	salt to taste
3 cups cooked and chilled rice	black pepper to taste

QUAIL

12 Manchester Farms semi-boneless quail	1/4 cup melted butter
kosher salt to taste	1/2 cup white wine
white pepper to taste	1/2 cup Chicken Stock (page 130)

METHOD

1. For the stuffing, sauté sausage in a sauté pan 5 minutes. Add remaining ingredients; mix well. Sauté lightly and cool to room temperature.

2. For the quail, preheat oven to 400 degrees. Stuff quail with the stuffing mixture and secure the cavities with wooden toothpicks. Season with salt and pepper. Place in a roasting pan and drizzle with butter. Roast 15 to 20 minutes or till cooked through.

3. Remove quail to a serving platter. Add wine to the roasting pan, stirring to de-glaze bottom of the pan. Add Chicken Stock and cook on the stove top till reduced to desired thickness. Serve over quail.

It is worth the extra effort to find Manchester Farms semi-boneless quail. They are larger than most, very clean and consistent in size.

GARLIC ROASTED CHICKEN WITH LEMON AND PEPPER

INGREDIENTS ———————————— Serves 4

1	whole chicken
2	tablespoons olive oil
1	lemon
	kosher salt to taste
	cracked black pepper to taste
2	coarsely chopped yellow onions
10	whole garlic cloves
1/4	cup chopped fresh parsley
1/4	cup grated Reggiano cheese

METHOD

1. Preheat oven to 450 degrees. Cut the chicken into quarters or eighths. Place skin side up in a roasting pan and drizzle with oil.

2. Peel the lemon and cut into thin slices, discarding the ends. Arrange slices on chicken; season with salt and pepper. Sprinkle onions and garlic in roasting pan, but do not cover the chicken heavily with onions.

3. Roast 20 to 25 minutes or till cooked through, testing the center of the thickest piece for doneness. Serve with roasted onions and garlic. Top with the pan juices, parsley and cheese.

CHICKEN SOFT TACOS

INGREDIENTS ———————————— Serves 4

1 1/2	pounds boneless chicken, beef or fish
1/4	cup Original Chef's Grill Plus
8	soft taco shells
3	cups shredded lettuce
1	cup chopped tomato
1	cup shredded Monterey Jack cheese
1/2	cup sour cream

METHOD

1. Preheat a grill surface to high. Brush the chicken with the Chef's Grill Plus and grill till cooked through. Cut into thin slices.

2. Warm taco shells using package directions. Top the shells with the chicken, lettuce, tomato, cheese and sour cream. Roll to enclose the filling. Omit cheese when using fish.

Always rise from the table with an appetite and you will never sit down without one.
—William Penn

1/2 cup = 4 oz • 1 gal = 4 qts = 8 pts = 16 cups = 128 oz • 1 qt = 4 cups = 32 oz • 1 pt = 16 oz = 2 cups

SEAFOOD

Cooking a memorable seafood dish is fun and simple. First, always buy fresh product. You can determine most seafood's quality by appearance and smell. When choosing fish it's difficult unless you can see the whole fish. A good rule of thumb is that the eye of the fish should be clear and bright—not cloudy—and the fish scales should be firm. It should be true to color and have little or no "fish smell." In many cases frozen products are acceptable. For example, shrimp and oysters for cooking freeze quite well. Pasteurized crabmeat is a great product, at times better than the fresh. Crawfish tails, raw oysters, lobster, clams and mussels must be fresh.

Remember, like many other food items that have regional counterparts, be resourceful and try to substitute the local equivalent of a product in a particular recipe. If you were in Hawaii, for example, you might choose Hebi in place of swordfish. Or if you were in California, you might substitute Dungeness Crab for Blue Crab.

Finally, the best way to ensure success is to select products from a familiar and reputable source. Once you do that, you can rest easy and concentrate on preparing the wonderful variety of seafood recipes in this book.

CEDAR PLANK-ROASTED SALMON

1	(14-inch) cedar plank	1/4	cup Original Chef's Grill Plus
1	(3-pound) side of fresh salmon	1	tablespoon chopped garlic
3	cups Chicken Stock (page 130)	1	cup brown sugar
1	tablespoon lemon juice	4	fresh rosemary sprigs
1/2	stick butter, chopped		

METHOD

1. Soak the plank in water for 30 minutes or longer. Preheat an outdoor grill to high.

2. Remove the skin and pin bones from the salmon.

3. Combine the Chicken Stock and lemon juice in a saucepan; cook till thickened and reduced to desired consistency. Whisk in the butter gradually.

4. Drain the plank and place salmon skin side down on it. Brush with the Chef's Grill Plus; sprinkle with garlic and brown sugar. Place on the grill and cover. Grill till fish flakes easily.

5. Serve on the plank with prepared sauce. Garnish with rosemary.

I was introduced to this cooking technique in the British Virgin Islands while visiting my great friends Jim and Duane, proprietors of Destin Ice Seafood. The cedar plank definitely imparts a great flavor to whatever food you cook on it.

3 tsp = 1 tbsp • 2 tbsp = 1/8 cup • 4 tbsp = 1/4 cup • 5 tbsp + 1 tsp = 1/3 cup • 1 cup = 8 oz

POTATO AND HORSERADISH-CRUSTED GROUPER WITH SHERRY REDUCTION SAUCE

INGREDIENTS ──────────────────────────────────── Serves 6

SHERRY REDUCTION SAUCE

2	cups Chicken Stock (page 130)	1/4	cup oyster sauce
2	cups dry sherry	1	teaspoon chopped garlic

GARLIC SPINACH

1/3   cup Garlic Butter (below)
3   cups packed fresh spinach

FISH

6	(6-ounce) grouper fillets		black pepper to taste
6	lightly beaten egg whites	6	medium Idaho potatoes
1/4	cup horseradish	1/2	cup melted butter
	salt to taste		

METHOD

1. For the sauce, combine all 4 ingredients in a medium saucepan. Cook till reduced by 3/4. Keep warm.

2. For the spinach, heat Garlic Butter in a large sauté pan. Add spinach and cook till wilted. Keep warm.

3. For the fish, preheat oven to 450 degrees. Dip fillets into egg whites and coat with horseradish; season with salt and pepper. Peel and shred potatoes. Shape into 6 cakes. Preheat a large sauté pan over medium to high heat and add butter. Add potato cakes and sear till golden brown.

4. Place one fillet in the center of each cake and mold the edges around the fillet; turn over and place in baking dish. Bake 7 minutes or till fish tests done. Serve over Garlic Spinach and top with Sherry Reduction Sauce.

For Garlic Butter, melt one stick butter with 1/4 cup canola oil. Let cool and stir in one tablespoon chopped garlic; add salt and white pepper to taste. This versatile mixture can be used to sauté many items.

1/2 cup = 4 oz • 1 gal = 4 qts = 8 pts = 16 cups = 128 oz • 1 qt = 4 cups = 32 oz • 1 pt = 16 oz = 2 cups

GROUPER TEMPURA WITH CHINESE BLACK BEAN SAUCE

INGREDIENTS ──────────────────────────────────── Serves 4

CHINESE BLACK SAUCE

1/2	cup Chicken Stock (page 130)	1/4	cup sugar
1/4	cup soy sauce	1	teaspoon chopped garlic
2	tablespoons rice vinegar	1/2	teaspoon chopped gingerroot
1	tablespoon sherry	1/2	teaspoon crushed red pepper flakes
1	tablespoon sesame oil		pinch of black pepper
1	(6-ounce) can fermented black beans	1/2	cup slurry (50% cornstarch 50% water)

FISH

1/4	cup canola oil	4	egg whites
1/2	cup flour	4	(6-ounce) grouper fillets
1/2	cup cornstarch	1	cup shredded carrots

METHOD

1. For the sauce, combine the first 11 ingredients in a saucepan; mix well. Bring to a boil and stir in slurry gradually. Cook till thickened and smooth, stirring constantly.

2. For the fish, preheat the oil for frying. Mix flour and cornstarch in a bowl. Beat the egg whites in a bowl till foamy. Dip fillets into egg whites and coat with flour mixture. Deep-fry 7 to 10 minutes; drain. Top with prepared sauce and garnish with shredded carrots.

Be careful about reading health food books. You may die of a misprint.
—Mark Twain

GRILLED REDFISH WITH CRAWFISH COUSCOUS

INGREDIENTS ———————————— Serves 4

3   cups water
     salt to taste
1   cup uncooked couscous
1/4 stick butter
1/2 pound fresh (peeled) crawfish tail meat
1/4 cup chopped green onions
     black pepper to taste
4   (7-ounce) redfish fillets
4   tablespoons Lemon Pepper Chef's Grill Plus
2   tablespoons lemon juice
1/4 cup olive oil
3   tablespoons water

METHOD

1. Bring 3 cups water and salt to a boil in a saucepan. Stir in the couscous and remove from heat. Let stand 8 minutes.

2. Heat the butter in a sauté pan; add the crawfish tails, green onions, salt and pepper. Cook just till crawfish are heated through. Add to the couscous and toss gently to mix. Keep warm.

3. Preheat oven to 450 degrees and preheat a grill surface. Brush fillets with Chef's Grill Plus following instructions on the container. Grill just till the fillets are marked from the grill. Remove fillets to a baking pan and drizzle with lemon juice, olive oil and 3 tablespoons water. Bake 5 minutes. Spoon couscous onto serving plates and top with fish.

GROUPER SANDWICH WITH CHIPOTLE TARTAR SAUCE

INGREDIENTS ———————————— Serves 4

TARTAR SAUCE
1 1/2 cups mayonnaise
1/4   cup chopped celery
2   tablespoons chopped onion
1/4   cup pickle relish
       puréed chipotle pepper to taste

SANDWICH
4   (5-ounce) grouper fillets
4   tablespoons Lemon Pepper Chef's Grill Plus
4   toasted Kaiser rolls
1/2   cup thinly shredded Napa cabbage
4   tomato slices

METHOD

1. For the tartar sauce, combine all 5 ingredients in a bowl; mix well. Chill in the refrigerator for 3 hours.

2. For the fish, preheat a grill surface. Season the fillets with Chef's Grill Plus following instructions on the container. Grill till cooked through.

3. Place fillets on the Kaiser roll bottoms. Top with the cabbage, tomato, tartar sauce and roll tops. Serve with a pickle and chips or fries.

SALT AND FIVE-SPICE CRUSTED SALMON WITH $750 BRAISED ROMAINE AND MUSHROOM EEL SAUCE

MUSHROOM EEL SAUCE

1/2	cup prepared eel sauce
2	cups quartered domestic mushrooms
1	cup Chicken Stock (page 130)

1	teaspoon chopped garlic
1	teaspoon ground black pepper

FISH

1/4	cup canola oil
4	(7-ounce) salmon fillets
	kosher salt to taste

	Chinese five-spice to taste
1	recipe $750 Braised Romaine (page 81)

METHOD

1. For the sauce, combine all 5 ingredients in a saucepan; mix well. Cook till reduced by 1/3. Keep warm.

2. For the fish, preheat oven to 450 degrees. Heat the oil in an ovenproof sauté pan. Season salmon with salt and Chinese five-spice. Add to the sauté pan and sauté till well-browned on one side.

3. Turn salmon over and place sauté pan in the oven. Bake 7 minutes or to desired doneness. Serve with $750 Braised Romaine and sauce.

> *No human being, however great, or powerful, was ever so free as a fish.*
> *—John Ruskin*

3 tsp = 1 tbsp • 2 tbsp = 1/8 cup • 4 tbsp = 1/4 cup • 5 tbsp + 1 tsp = 1/3 cup • 1 cup = 8 oz

CRISPY FRIED SOFT-SHELL CRABS WITH CHINESE BARBECUE SAUCE

INGREDIENTS ——————— Serves 4

1/2	cup oyster sauce
1/4	cup rice vinegar
2	tablespoons ketchup
3	drops sesame oil
1	teaspoon chopped garlic
1/4	cup sugar
1	teaspoon Chinese five-spice
	canola oil for frying
1/4	cup Original Chef's Grill Plus
1/2	cup milk
4	cleaned jumbo soft-shell crabs
2	cups corn flour
1/4	cup chopped green onions

METHOD

1. Combine the first 7 ingredients in a small saucepan; mix well. Bring to a boil and remove from heat; keep warm.

2. Heat canola oil to 350 degrees in a deep fryer or electric skillet. Mix the Chef's Grill Plus and milk in a small bowl. Dip the crabs in the milk wash and coat with the corn flour, shaking off the excess.

3. Place crabs belly side up in the heated oil and fry about 6 minutes or till golden brown and very crisp; drain on paper towels. Serve crabs belly side up. Drizzle with sauce and garnish with green onions.

TUNA STEAKS WITH BONIATO CAKES AND WATERMELON SALSA

INGREDIENTS ——————— Serves 4

1 1/2	cups Mashed Boniato (page 79)
2	beaten egg whites
1	cup bread crumbs
	canola oil for frying
4	(6-ounce) tuna steaks
4	tablespoons Original Chef's Grill Plus
1	recipe Watermelon-Pineapple Salsa (page 141)

METHOD

1. Shape the Mashed Boniato into 4 cakes. Dip cakes into egg whites and then into the bread crumbs. Heat the oil to 350 degrees in a deep fryer or electric skillet. Add cakes and fry till brown and crisp. Keep warm.

2. Preheat a grill surface. Brush the tuna steaks with the Chef's Grill Plus, following the instructions on the container. Grill till desired doneness. Serve over cakes. Top with salsa.

Fish should smell like the tide. Once they smell like fish, it's too late.
—Oscar Gizelt, of Delmonico's restaurant, New York, Vogue, 1964

1/2 cup = 4 oz • 1 gal = 4 qts = 8 pts = 16 cups = 128 oz • 1 qt = 4 cups = 32 oz • 1 pt = 16 oz = 2 cups

FLORIDA LOBSTER WITH HONEY-LIME-RUM GLAZE

INGREDIENTS ———————————————————————————— Serves 4

1/2	cup Key lime juice		salt to taste
1	tablespoon cornstarch		ground black pepper to taste
1/2	cup Myers dark rum	4	(8-ounce) Florida lobster tails
3/4	cup honey	4	tablespoons Original Chef's Grill Plus
1	tablespoon chopped pickled ginger	1/4	cup chopped fresh basil

METHOD

1. Combine 2 tablespoons lime juice with the cornstarch; set aside. Combine remaining lime juice with rum, honey and ginger; bring to a boil. Add the cornstarch mixture and boil briefly. Season with salt and pepper.

2. Preheat a grill surface to high. Split lobster tails and remove meat, leaving the end of the tail connected. Stuff meat back in the shell. Brush the exposed meat lightly with Chef's Grill Plus. Grill for about 7 minutes or to desired doneness.

3. Add basil to the sauce. Serve lobster with the prepared sauce.

Ruling a big country is like cooking a small fish.
—Lao-Tzu

3 tsp = 1 tbsp • 2 tbsp = 1/8 cup • 4 tbsp = 1/4 cup • 5 tbsp + 1 tsp = 1/3 cup • 1 cup = 8 oz

FRIED LOBSTER WITH MASHED BONIATO AND KEY LIME MUSTARD AÏOLI

KEY LIME MUSTARD AÏOLI

1/4	cup Dijon mustard	2	tablespoons sour cream
1/4	cup mayonnaise	1	tablespoon Key lime juice

LOBSTER

4	(1 1/2-pound) Maine lobsters	3/4	recipe Mashed Boniato (page 79)
	canola oil for frying	2	chopped green onions
5	egg whites	1	quartered lemon
1 1/2	cups bread crumbs	1	quartered lime
1 1/2	cups corn flour	1	tablespoon cayenne pepper

METHOD

1. For the aïoli, combine all 4 ingredients in a bowl; mix till smooth.

2. For the lobster, steam and remove meat from the shells. Heat the oil to 350 degrees in a deep fryer or electric skillet. Beat the egg whites in a bowl till frothy. Mix bread crumbs and corn flour in a bowl.

3. Dip lobster into egg whites and coat with bread crumb mixture. Fry in heated oil for 4 to 5 minutes or till golden brown and crisp; drain on paper towels.

4. Serve lobster over Mashed Boniato and drizzle with aïoli. Garnish with remaining ingredients.

Fish and visitors smell in three days.
—Benjamin Franklin

1/2 cup = 4 oz • 1 gal = 4 qts = 8 pts = 16 cups = 128 oz • 1 qt = 4 cups = 32 oz • 1 pt = 16 oz = 2 cups

SPICY THAI MUSSELS

1	tablespoon butter	80	mussels
1/2	chopped yellow onion	1/4	cup chopped cilantro
2	tablespoons chopped garlic	1/2	(8-ounce) can coconut milk
1	chopped jalapeno	1	tablespoon lime juice
1	chopped tomato		salt to taste
1/4	cup white wine		black pepper to taste
2	tablespoons tomato paste		

METHOD

1. Heat the butter in a large sauté pan. Add the next 4 ingredients; sauté briefly. Stir in wine and tomato paste. Add the next 4 ingredients. Cover and steam till all the mussel shells open.

2. Remove mussels to a serving dish with a slotted spoon. Cook sauce till reduced to desired consistency. Season with salt and pepper. Serve over mussels.

Fresh Prince Edward Island mussels are a great selection for this recipe.

3 tsp = 1 tbsp • 2 tbsp = 1/8 cup • 4 tbsp = 1/4 cup • 5 tbsp + 1 tsp = 1/3 cup • 1 cup = 8 oz

HABANERO-SPICED GRILLED GULF SHRIMP

HABANERO SAUCE

3	finely chopped habanero peppers		3	tablespoons water
1/2	cup soy sauce		3	tablespoons sugar
1/4	cup white vinegar		2	teaspoons chopped gingerroot
3	tablespoons tomato paste		2	teaspoons chopped garlic

SHRIMP

20	peeled (16-20 count) Gulf shrimp		1/4	cup Habanero Chef's Grill Plus

METHOD

1. For the sauce, combine all 8 ingredients in a saucepan; bring to a low boil. Boil for 5 minutes. Reduce heat and keep warm.

2. Preheat a grill surface. Toss shrimp with the Chef's Grill Plus and grill till cooked through. Serve with sauce.

Hunger is the best sauce in the world.
—Miguel de Cervantes

1/2 cup = 4 oz • 1 gal = 4 qts = 8 pts = 16 cups = 128 oz • 1 qt = 4 cups = 32 oz • 1 pt = 16 oz = 2 cups

STOCKS & SAUCES

Stocks and sauces have always held a special place in my cooking. After realizing that my true calling was to be a chef, my mentor, Chef Parola, taught me that the base of all great food is the use of properly made stocks and sauces. He taught me that you don't have to use a lot of fancy ingredients when you're creating either. The ingredients can be extremely simple, allowing meats and vegetables to shine naturally.

I also learned that preparing stocks and sauces from scratch is quickly becoming a lost art. Because of the time and care involved, many never learn how to make these great base ingredients. I go to great lengths to create the perfect stock or sauce. It's not unusual for me to create five or six sauces before I find the perfect one for a particular dish. Too much of that, not enough of this—it can take a while, but believe me, once I have found the right combination of ingredients and flavors, it's well worth the effort.

Don't be intimidated; most basic stocks can be prepared from simple ingredients. In fact, many of the ingredients used in creating stocks are by-products. Onion tops and peelings, tomato skins and hulls, carcasses from roasted poultry, bones from fish and meat, the remains of chopped parsley and other fresh herbs, all can be utilized nicely in stocks.

As Chef Parola taught me, stocks and sauces are the true cornerstones of cooking. Without them, a meal can be as uneventful as a cake without icing.

CHICKEN STOCK

1	large yellow onion	1/2	gallon white wine
1	celery rib	2	sprigs fresh thyme
1 1/2	large carrots	1	bay leaf
2	chicken carcasses	1/2	tablespoon ground white pepper
1	garlic bulb	4	tablespoons salt
1	sprig fresh parsley		

METHOD

1. Cut onion, celery and carrots into large pieces. Combine the chopped vegetables and remaining ingredients with enough water to fill a 5-gallon stockpot within 4 inches of the top. Bring to a slow rolling boil.

2. Cook for 2 hours, skimming surface frequently. Remove from heat and strain through a fine sieve or chinois. Let stand till cool.

It is better to remain silent than speak the truth ill-humouredly, and so spoil an excellent dish by covering it with a bad sauce.
—Jean-Pierre Camus

3 tsp = 1 tbsp • 2 tbsp = 1/8 cup • 4 tbsp = 1/4 cup • 5 tbsp + 1 tsp = 1/3 cup • 1 cup = 8 oz

DUCK STOCK

4	duck carcasses		2	cups red wine
1 1/2	large yellow onions		1/2	cup white wine
1	celery rib		1	cup tomato paste
1 1/2	large carrots		1	tablespoon black peppercorns
	leftover duck meat (optional)		2	sprigs fresh thyme
1 1/2	garlic bulbs		2	bay leaves
1	sprig fresh parsley		2	tablespoons salt

METHOD

1. Preheat oven to 450 degrees. Place the bones on a baking sheet and roast till brown on all sides. Cut the onions, celery and carrots into large pieces. Combine the chopped vegetables, bones, meat and remaining ingredients with enough water to fill a 5-gallon stockpot within 4 inches of the top. Bring to a slow rolling boil.

2. Cook 6 hours, skimming surface frequently. Remove from heat and strain through a fine sieve or chinois. Let stand till cool.

What is sauce for the goose may be sauce for the gander, but it is not necessarily sauce for the chicken, the duck, the turkey or Guinea hen.
—Alice B. Toklas

1/2 cup = 4 oz • 1 gal = 4 qts = 8 pts = 16 cups = 128 oz • 1 qt = 4 cups = 32 oz • 1 pt = 16 oz = 2 cups

FISH STOCK

1	large yellow onion	2	cups white wine
1	celery rib	1/2	cup dry vermouth
1 1/2	large carrots	1	sprig fresh thyme
1/4	cup olive oil	2	whole cloves
3	pounds fish bones (no heads)	2	bay leaves
1	sprig fresh parsley	1	teaspoon black peppercorns
1/2	cup sherry	3	tablespoons salt

METHOD

1. Cut onion, celery and carrots into large pieces. Heat oil in a heavy 5-gallon stockpot. Add the bones and cook till the meat is white. Add the vegetables and remaining ingredients and enough water to fill the stockpot within 4 inches of the top. Bring to a rapid boil. Cook one hour, skimming surface frequently. Remove from heat.

2. Strain through a fine sieve or chinois. Return the strained stock to stockpot. Bring to a slow boil. Cook one hour longer. Let stand till cool.

In England there are sixty different religions, and only one sauce.
—Francesco Caraccioli

3 tsp = 1 tbsp • 2 tbsp = 1/8 cup • 4 tbsp = 1/4 cup • 5 tbsp + 1 tsp = 1/3 cup • 1 cup = 8 oz

LOBSTER STOCK

5	Maine lobster shells and heads		1	cup brandy
1	large yellow onion		1	cup tomato paste
1	celery rib		1	sprig fresh parsley
1 1/2	large carrots		4	sprigs fresh thyme
1/4	cup olive oil		1	tablespoon black peppercorns
1	garlic pod		2	bay leaves
2	cups white wine		2	tablespoons salt
1/2	cup sherry			

METHOD

1. Chop the shells, onion, celery and carrots into large pieces. Heat oil in a large braising pan. Add the chopped ingredients and cook till vegetables are light brown.

2. Remove to a heavy 5-gallon stockpot. Add remaining ingredients and enough water to fill the stockpot within 4 inches of the top. Bring to a rapid boil. Cook for 2 hours, skimming surface frequently. Remove from heat.

3. Strain through a fine sieve or chinois. Return strained stock to the stockpot and bring to a slow boil. Cook one hour longer. Let stand till cool.

Bait the hook well; this fish will bite.
—William Shakespeare

1/2 cup = 4 oz • 1 gal = 4 qts = 8 pts = 16 cups = 128 oz • 1 qt = 4 cups = 32 oz • 1 pt = 16 oz = 2 cups

VEAL STOCK AND VEAL GLACE

INGREDIENTS ———————————————————— Makes about 2 gallons stock or 3/4 gallon glace

2	pounds veal or beef bones	1/2	(10-ounce) can peeled whole tomatoes
1/4	cup flour	1	gallon red wine
1	large yellow onion	1	cup white wine
1	celery rib	4	sprigs fresh thyme
1 1/2	large carrots	1	bay leaf
1/2	garlic bulb	1	teaspoon black peppercorns
1	sprig fresh parsley	2	cups red wine (for glace only), add last

METHOD

1. Preheat oven to 350 degrees. Crack bones to expose marrow and place on a baking sheet. Dust lightly with flour. Roast till bones and meat are brown. Place in a heavy 5-gallon stockpot.

2. Cut the onion, celery and carrots into large pieces. Place in stockpot. Add the next 8 ingredients and enough water to fill the stockpot within 4 inches of the top. Bring to a slow rolling boil. Cook 24 hours, skimming surface frequently. Remove from heat. Strain through a fine sieve or chinois. Let stand till cool. May be thickened with 2 cups of roux to make brown sauce.

3. For the glace: You should have about 3 gallons. Return strained stock to the stockpot and add 2 cups red wine. Bring to a medium boil. Cook till reduced by 2/3, skimming surface frequently.

Blonde Roux: 50% butter or oil and 50% flour, blended well. Boil 5 minutes, stirring continuously.

3 tsp = 1 tbsp • 2 tbsp = 1/8 cup • 4 tbsp = 1/4 cup • 5 tbsp + 1 tsp = 1/3 cup • 1 cup = 8 oz

VEGETABLE STOCK

INGREDIENTS ———————— Makes about 2 gallons

4	large yellow onions
4	celery ribs
5	large carrots
1/4	cup olive oil
2	garlic bulbs
2	cups white wine
4	tomatoes, cut into large pieces
2	sprigs fresh parsley
2	tablespoons fresh thyme leaves
2	bay leaves
2	tablespoons black peppercorns
1/4	cup salt

METHOD

1. Cut onions, celery and carrots into large pieces. Heat oil in a heavy 5-gallon stockpot and add the chopped vegetables. Sauté till light brown. Add the remaining ingredients and enough water to fill the stockpot within 4 inches of the top.

2. Bring to a rapid boil. Cook one hour. Remove from heat. Strain through a fine sieve or chinois. Let stand till cool.

FISH FUMET WITH MUSHROOMS

INGREDIENTS ———————— Makes 8 cups

2	cups Fish Stock or Chicken Stock (pages 132 or 130)
1/4	cup dry vermouth
1/4	cup heavy cream
6	medium mushrooms, sliced
1/4	cup finely chopped tomato
	pinch of chopped garlic
1	tablespoon chopped fresh parsley
2	teaspoons lemon juice
1	tablespoon Blonde Roux (page 134)
	salt to taste
	black pepper to taste

METHOD

1. Combine the first 8 ingredients in a heavy saucepan; bring to a boil.

2. Stir in Roux slowly. Bring to a simmer, stirring constantly. Simmer 20 minutes. Season with salt and pepper.

Without bread, without wine, love is nothing.
—French Proverb

CHIPOTLE SAUCE

INGREDIENTS ———————— Makes 1 1/2 cups

1/3 cup **Veal Glace** (page 134)
1/3 cup **Chicken Stock** (page 130)
     pinch of chopped garlic
1/2 chipotle pepper in adobo sauce
2   tablespoons tomato paste
     salt to taste
2/3 cup sour cream

METHOD

1. Combine first 6 ingredients in a saucepan. Bring to a simmer and reduce by half.

2. Remove from heat. Process with a hand mixer till smooth. Whisk in sour cream.

BÉCHAMEL SAUCE

INGREDIENTS ———————— Makes 5 cups

2   cups heavy cream
2   cups milk
1/4 cup **Blonde Roux** (page 134)
1/4 cup dry sherry
1   teaspoon ground nutmeg
     salt to taste
     white pepper to taste

METHOD

1. Bring cream and milk to a boil in a heavy saucepan. Stir in Roux. Add sherry. Bring to a boil, stirring constantly. Reduce heat and simmer 30 minutes.

2. Stir in nutmeg and season with salt and pepper. Stir in additional milk if the sauce is too thick. Strain through a fine sieve or chinois.

Mayonnaise: One of the sauces which serve the French in place of a state religion.
—Ambrose Bierce

3 tsp = 1 tbsp • 2 tbsp = 1/8 cup • 4 tbsp = 1/4 cup • 5 tbsp + 1 tsp = 1/3 cup • 1 cup = 8 oz

CILANTRO CREAM

INGREDIENTS —————————— Makes I cup

1/2 cup sour cream
I   teaspoon lime juice
1/2 bunch cilantro
    salt to taste

METHOD

1. Combine first 3 ingredients in a food processor; process till smooth.

2. Spoon into a bowl and season with salt. Cover and chill till serving time.

TARRAGON CREAM SAUCE

INGREDIENTS —————————— Makes I cup

I   cup heavy cream
2   tablespoons white wine
I   teaspoon tarragon vinegar
I   tablespoon tomato paste
I   teaspoon chopped garlic
2   teaspoons tarragon leaves
    salt to taste
    white pepper to taste

METHOD

1. Combine first 6 ingredients in a saucepan; bring to a slow boil.

2. Cook till reduced to desired consistency. Season with salt and pepper.

Cooking is at once child's play and adult joy. And, cooking done with care is an act of love.
—Craig Claiborne

STEAK SAUCE

INGREDIENTS ───────────── Serves 4

1/2   cup Veal Stock (page 134)
I   tablespoon butter
      pinch of chopped garlic
I   teaspoon Worcestershire sauce
I   teaspoon soy sauce

METHOD

1.   Combine all ingredients in a saucepan. Bring
     to a simmer.

2.   Remove from heat and pour into a storage
     container. Store in refrigerator.

MARINARA SAUCE VIGNONE

INGREDIENTS ───────────── Serves 8

2   tablespoons olive oil
1/2   large chopped yellow onion
4   chopped garlic cloves
4   cups peeled Italian plum tomatoes with juice
1/3   cup tomato paste
1/2   cup grated Romano cheese
1/2   cup chopped basil
      black pepper to taste

METHOD

1.   Heat oil in a saucepan. Add onion and
     garlic; sauté 5 minutes. Pass tomatoes
     through a food mill; discard pulp. Add to
     the onion mixture. Bring to a slow boil.

2.   Stir in remaining ingredients. Simmer
     30 minutes. Adjust seasonings if needed.

*Make hunger thy sauce, as a medicine
for health.*
—Thomas Tusser

3 tsp = I tbsp • 2 tbsp = 1/8 cup • 4 tbsp = 1/4 cup • 5 tbsp + I tsp = 1/3 cup • I cup = 8 oz

SOY DIPPING SAUCE

INGREDIENTS —————— Serves 4

3	tablespoons soy sauce
2	tablespoons rice vinegar
I	tablespoon sugar
3	drops sesame oil
1/4	teaspoon chopped garlic
1/2	teaspoon Thai chile paste
I	teaspoon minced scallions

METHOD

1. Combine all ingredients in a bowl; mix well.

2. Store covered in the refrigerator till serving time.

CARAMELIZED ONION AÏOLI

INGREDIENTS —————— Serves 8

I	tablespoon butter
1/2	julienned yellow onion
1/2	teaspoon chopped garlic
I	cup sour cream
1/4	cup chopped green onions
	salt to taste
	black pepper to taste

METHOD

1. Melt butter in a large sauté pan. Add onion and sauté till dark and caramelized, taking care not to burn. Remove from heat and let stand till cool.

2. Combine onion with garlic, sour cream and onions in a blender; process till smooth. Season with salt and pepper.

Part of the secret of success in life is to eat what you like and let the food fight it out inside.
—Mark Twain

SWEET CORN AND CRAB MEAT SAUCE

INGREDIENTS ———————— Serves 8

1/2   stick butter
1/4   large finely chopped onion
2   teaspoons chopped garlic
2   cups fresh corn kernels
2   tablespoons flour
3/4   cup Chicken Stock (page 130)
1   cup heavy cream
3   chopped green onions
     salt to taste
     black pepper to taste
1 1/2   teaspoons lemon juice
1/2   cup jumbo lump crab meat

METHOD

1. Melt the butter in a heavy saucepan. Add the onion, garlic and corn; sauté 5 minutes. Stir in flour and cook till bubbly. Add the Chicken Stock gradually, stirring constantly. Bring to a slow boil, stirring constantly till thickened and smooth. Cook 25 minutes.

2. Pour into a blender and process till smooth. Add cream and onions. Season with salt and pepper. Add lemon juice and crab meat just before serving. Adjust thickness with additional Chicken Stock.

BALSAMIC GLAZE

INGREDIENTS ———————— Makes 1/2 cup

1/4   cup balsamic vinegar
2   tablespoons honey

METHOD

1. Combine vinegar and honey in a small saucepan. Cook over medium heat till very thick. Cool to room temperature.

2. Stir in a small amount of water if sauce is too thick. Chill covered till ready to use.

The cook was a good cook, as cooks go; and as cooks go, she went.
—Saki

3 tsp = 1 tbsp • 2 tbsp = 1/8 cup • 4 tbsp = 1/4 cup • 5 tbsp + 1 tsp = 1/3 cup • 1 cup = 8 oz

PINEAPPLE AND BABY BEAN SALSA

I	peeled and sliced pineapple
3	tablespoons canola oil
I	tablespoon ground chipotle pepper
I	tablespoon kosher salt
1/2	chopped yellow onion
I	tablespoon chopped garlic
1/2	chopped jalapeno
2	cups cut baby green beans (haricots verts)
3	chopped tomatoes
I	cup rice vinegar
1/2	cup pineapple juice
I	tablespoon turmeric powder
	salt to taste

METHOD

1. Preheat the grill. Arrange pineapple slices in a single layer in a shallow dish. Combine oil, pepper and kosher salt in a bowl; mix well. Pour over pineapple slices. Marinate 5 minutes. Drain, reserving the marinade. Grill pineapple slices briefly. Remove from grill. Remove core and chop the slices.

2. Combine pineapple, reserved marinade and next 8 ingredients in a saucepan. Bring to a boil. Reduce heat and simmer 15 minutes. Season with salt. Serve warm.

WATERMELON-PINEAPPLE SALSA

I	cup chopped and seeded watermelon
I	cup chopped pineapple
2	tablespoons chopped cilantro
1/2	cup chopped red onion
2	tablespoons rice wine vinegar
	salt to taste
	black pepper to taste

METHOD

1. Combine all ingredients in a large bowl; mix well.

2. Store covered in the refrigerator till serving time, or up to 2 days. Serve on grilled fish or seafood.

Before you trust a man, eat a peck of salt with him.
—Proverb

MANGO BARBECUE SAUCE

INGREDIENTS ———————————— Makes 2 cups

1	tablespoon Dijon mustard
1	tablespoon chopped garlic
1/2	chopped jalapeno
2	cups mango purée
1	tablespoon brown sugar
2	tablespoons tomato sauce
2	tablespoons Veal Glace (page 134)

METHOD

1. Combine all ingredients in a saucepan. Bring to a simmer.

2. Cook 35 minutes.

3. Store covered in refrigerator till ready to use.

MANGO CHUTNEY

INGREDIENTS ———————————— Serves 6

2	chopped mangoes
1/2	cup chopped red onion
1/4	cup golden raisins
1	teaspoon chopped garlic
2	tablespoons brown sugar
2	tablespoons Worcestershire sauce
	crushed red pepper to taste

METHOD

1. Combine all ingredients in a bowl; mix well. Process half the mixture in a food processor till smooth.

2. Combine purée with remaining mango mixture and mix well. Cover and chill till serving time.

Bad men live that they may eat and drink, whereas good men eat and drink that they may live.
—Socrates

3 tsp = 1 tbsp • 2 tbsp = 1/8 cup • 4 tbsp = 1/4 cup • 5 tbsp + 1 tsp = 1/3 cup • 1 cup = 8 oz

PICO DE GALLO

INGREDIENTS ———————————— Serves 4

1	chopped tomato
1	chopped jalapeno
1/2	large chopped yellow onion
1/2	bunch cilantro, chopped
1	teaspoon salt
1	tablespoon white vinegar

METHOD

1. Combine all ingredients in a bowl; mix well.

2. Store covered in refrigerator till serving time.

GRILLED VEGETABLE SALSA

INGREDIENTS ———————————— Serves 4

2	ears corn
1	bunch green onions
1	red bell pepper
2	tablespoons Original Chef's Grill Plus
1	tablespoon chopped cilantro
	juice of 1/2 lime
1	cup chopped tomato
	salt to taste
	black pepper to taste

METHOD

1. Preheat grill. Brush corn, onions and bell pepper lightly with Chef's Grill Plus. Grill till charred, turning constantly. Remove from grill. Cut corn kernels from cobs and chop onions and bell pepper finely. Place in bowl.

2. Add cilantro, lime juice and tomato; mix well. Season with salt and pepper.

I never eat in a restaurant that's over a hundred feet off the ground and won't stand still.
—Calvin Trillin

RASPBERRY COULIS

INGREDIENTS ———————————— Serves 4

2 pints fresh raspberries
1 cup confectioners' sugar
1/2 cup water

METHOD

1. Combine raspberries, sugar and water in a blender; process till smooth. Spoon into a saucepan and bring to a boil over medium heat. Boil 10 minutes.

2. Remove from heat and press through a fine sieve or chinois, adding additional water if needed for desired consistency. Chill till serving time.

BUTTERSCOTCH SAUCE

INGREDIENTS ———————————— Makes 4 cups

2 cups packed brown sugar
2/3 cup corn syrup
1/2 cup water
1 stick butter
1 cup heavy cream
1/2 cup sour cream
1 tablespoon vanilla extract
    pinch of salt

METHOD

1. Combine the first 4 ingredients in a saucepan; bring to a boil. Cook 4 minutes or to 236 degrees on a candy thermometer, soft-ball stage, stirring frequently.

2. Remove from heat and let stand till slightly cooled. Add remaining ingredients; beat well till thickened to desired consistency. Serve warm or cold.

Politics is applesauce.
—Will Rogers

3 tsp = 1 tbsp • 2 tbsp = 1/8 cup • 4 tbsp = 1/4 cup • 5 tbsp + 1 tsp = 1/3 cup • 1 cup = 8 oz

CARAMEL SAUCE

INGREDIENTS ———————— Serves 10

1	cup sugar
2	tablespoons water
3/4	cup heavy cream
1/2	stick butter
1	teaspoon vanilla extract
	pinch of salt

METHOD

1. Combine sugar and water in a saucepan; mix well. Bring to a boil over medium heat. Cook till mixture is amber in color. Remove from heat and whisk in cream.

2. Add butter, vanilla and salt; mix well. Let stand till cool. Cover and store at room temperature.

CHOCOLATE SAUCE

INGREDIENTS ———————— Serves 10

8	ounces semi-sweet chocolate
1	cup heavy cream

METHOD

1. Combine chocolate and cream in a microwave-safe bowl or double boiler.

2. Microwave on low or heat over simmering water till the chocolate melts, stirring occasionally.

The time-honored bread sauce of the happy ending.
—Henry James

1/2 cup = 4 oz • 1 gal = 4 qts = 8 pts = 16 cups = 128 oz • 1 qt = 4 cups = 32 oz • 1 pt = 16 oz = 2 cups

TRIED & TRUE

The Tried & True chapter is one of my favorites because it features a dozen of the most-requested recipes from *Flavors of the Gulf Coast*, my first cookbook, as well as from my classes and latest menus. While some chefs are reluctant to share their recipes with others on request, I take a different approach: if someone asks me for a recipe for a particular dish, I'm always happy to share it. In my mind, there is no bigger compliment—giving to others is what it's all about!

My desire to share my joy is why the majority of the recipes in this book are simple to prepare and made from easy-to-find ingredients. I tell our guests at my restaurant, and the students who take my cooking classes, that cooking and enjoyment shouldn't be a contradiction in terms. Cooking should be easy— and fun! It ought to be a time where friends and family come together to create special memories.

Everyone seems to have a favorite dish that reminds them of a special time or place or someone special in their life. Or it may have been they prepared a dish "from scratch"—something simple and easy to prepare, but a dish that gave them a great sense of personal satisfaction that makes it their favorite.

I am often surprised to learn which of my recipes have become others' favorites. I'm happy knowing that my customers and students *do* have favorites— and that I get the pleasure of sharing my own joy of cooking with them. And, I hope, with you!

CRISPY KUNG PAO OYSTERS

KUNG PAO SAUCE

1/4	cup oyster sauce
1/4	cup soy sauce
2	tablespoons sherry
1	tablespoon rice vinegar
2	tablespoons chopped green onions
1	tablespoon sugar

2	teaspoons chopped garlic
1	teaspoon chopped gingerroot
1	tablespoon cornstarch
1/4	cup water
	crushed red pepper flakes to taste

OYSTERS

	canola oil for frying
32	oysters on the half shell
2	cups corn flour

1	thinly sliced red onion
1	tablespoon poppy seeds

METHOD

1. For the sauce, combine the first 8 ingredients in a saucepan; mix well. Bring to a low boil. Blend cornstarch with the water in a small bowl and stir into boiling sauce. Return to a low boil and season with pepper. Keep warm.

2. For the oysters, preheat oil to 350 degrees in a deep fryer or electric skillet. Remove oysters from shells; reserve shells. Coat the oysters with corn flour. Fry in heated oil 4 minutes or till very crisp.

3. Place oysters back in the reserved shells and top with the Kung Pao Sauce and onion. Sprinkle with poppy seeds.

Never serve oysters in a month that has no paycheck in it.
—P.J. O'Rourke

3 tsp = 1 tbsp • 2 tbsp = 1/8 cup • 4 tbsp = 1/4 cup • 5 tbsp + 1 tsp = 1/3 cup • 1 cup = 8 oz

THREE-CHEESE BAKED OYSTERS

INGREDIENTS ——————————— Serves 4

1/4 cup chopped prosciutto
1   teaspoon chopped garlic
1   tablespoon olive oil
1/2 cup heavy cream
1   cup shredded Fontina cheese
1   cup grated Romano cheese
1   tablespoon Crystal hot sauce
32   oysters on the half shell
1/2 cup shredded Housemade Mozzarella (page 67)
3/4 cup bread crumbs

METHOD

1. Sauté prosciutto and garlic in heated oil in a sauté pan for 3 minutes. Add the next 4 ingredients; mix well. Simmer just till cheeses melt; stir to mix well. Remove from heat and cool to room temperature.

2. Preheat oven to 450 degrees. Arrange oysters on the shells in a baking pan. Sprinkle each oyster with mozzarella cheese. Top with 2 tablespoons of sauce and a sprinkle of bread crumbs. Bake 8 minutes or till edges of oysters curl.

MARINATED CRAB CLAWS

INGREDIENTS ——————————— Serves 4

1/2 cup olive oil
1/2 cup red wine vinegar
1   bunch green onions
3   tablespoons Worcestershire sauce
1/2 bunch parsley
1/2 celery rib
1/4 cup green olives
4   garlic cloves
     salt to taste
     black pepper to taste
1   pound cooked crab claws

METHOD

1. Combine the first 10 ingredients in a food processor; process till smooth. Add crab claws. Marinate 2 hours or more in the refrigerator.

2. Drain crab claws, reserving the marinade. Arrange crab claws on a serving plate and top with reserved marinade.

Many's the long night I've dreamed of cheese—toasted, mostly.
—*Robert Louis Stevenson*

1/2 cup = 4 oz • 1 gal = 4 qts = 8 pts = 16 cups = 128 oz • 1 qt = 4 cups = 32 oz • 1 pt = 16 oz = 2 cups

SEAFOOD BISQUE

1	stick butter	1/2	cup baby shrimp
1/2	chopped onion	1/2	cup crab meat
1	tablespoon chopped garlic	1	cup clams with liquid
1/2	chopped celery rib	1	cup chopped fish
1	cup crushed Italian plum tomatoes	1	teaspoon lemon juice
1/2	cup flour	1/2	bunch green onions, chopped
1/4	cup sherry	1	teaspoon paprika
1	cup white wine		salt to taste
2	cups heavy cream		black pepper to taste
1	quart milk		cayenne pepper to taste
1/2	cup scallops	2	tablespoons chopped basil
1/2	cup fresh (peeled) crawfish tail meat		

METHOD

1. Melt butter in a heavy bottomed soup pot. Add the next 4 ingredients and sauté 10 minutes. Stir in flour and cook till bubbly. Add sherry, wine, cream and milk; bring to a low boil, stirring constantly.

2. Add the next 6 ingredients. Stir in lemon juice, green onions and paprika; return to a low boil.

3. Simmer 20 minutes. Season with salt, black pepper and cayenne pepper. Ladle into soup bowls. Garnish with chopped basil.

It's good food and not fine words that keeps me alive.
—Jean Baptiste Molière

HOT CRAWFISH SALAD

INGREDIENTS ———————————————————— Serves 8

DIJON VINAIGRETTE

1	egg yolk
1/4	cup red wine vinegar
3	tablespoons Dijon mustard
1	teaspoon salt
2	cups olive oil
1/2	chopped red onion

2	chopped green onions
1/2	chopped celery rib
1/2	chopped red bell pepper
1/2	chopped green bell pepper
	white pepper to taste

SALAD

	canola oil for frying
1/2	cup Original Chef's Grill Plus
1	cup milk
2	cups flour
1	pound fresh (peeled) crawfish tail meat

12	leaves Belgian endive
3	cups salad greens
2	sliced Roma tomatoes
1	julienned red bell pepper

METHOD

1. For the vinaigrette, combine first 4 ingredients in a blender; process till smooth. Add the oil gradually, processing constantly at high speed.

2. Combine mustard mixture with next 5 ingredients in a bowl; mix well. Season with white pepper and chill till serving time.

3. For the salad, preheat oil in a deep fryer or electric skillet to 350 degrees. Blend the Chef's Grill Plus and milk in a bowl; beat till smooth.

4. Dip crawfish tails into egg mixture and coat with flour, shaking off excess. Fry in heated oil 3 minutes or till golden brown; drain.

5. Line serving plates with Belgian endive and top with salad greens. Spoon crawfish tails over salad greens and top with vinaigrette. Garnish with tomatoes and bell pepper. Serve immediately.

1/2 cup = 4 oz • 1 gal = 4 qts = 8 pts = 16 cups = 128 oz • 1 qt = 4 cups = 32 oz • 1 pt = 16 oz = 2 cups

CELERY-GARLIC MASHED POTATOES

INGREDIENTS ———————————— Serves 6

5	Idaho baking potatoes
3	coarsely chopped celery ribs
1	cup heavy cream
1	stick butter
2	tablespoons chopped garlic
	salt to taste
	black pepper to taste

METHOD

1. Peel the potatoes and cut into 2-inch pieces. In a medium saucepan, cover potatoes with water and cook till tender. In a separate saucepan, cover celery with water and cook till tender.

2. Drain potatoes and celery. Place celery in a food processor or blender and process till smooth. Combine the potatoes and celery in a mixing bowl and beat till smooth. Add remaining ingredients; mix well.

FRIED TURKEY

INGREDIENTS ———————————— Serves 12

4	gallons peanut oil
1	(12-pound) turkey
	granulated garlic to taste
	paprika to taste
	salt to taste
	black pepper to taste

METHOD

1. Preheat the oil in a 10-gallon pot or a large deep fryer. Season turkey heavily inside and out with remaining ingredients.

2. Fry the turkey in an open area rather than in a confined area such as a garage. Heat oil 5 minutes for each pound, rolling over once during the process. Remove to paper towels to drain 15 minutes. Slice and serve immediately.

Tim Creehan is one of the most creative chefs practicing his craft in the United States today. His innovative dishes carry a touch of New Orleans and what I call Nouveau Gulf Coastal. I spent Thanksgiving at his signature restaurant and feasted on Fried Turkey! The best! It seals the juices and delivers the taste.
—*Wayne Rogers, Actor, M·A·S·H*

3 tsp = 1 tbsp • 2 tbsp = 1/8 cup • 4 tbsp = 1/4 cup • 5 tbsp + 1 tsp = 1/3 cup • 1 cup = 8 oz

SEARED YELLOWFIN TUNA

SOY GINGER SAUCE

1/4	cup soy sauce
1/4	cup rice vinegar
1	tablespoon water

1	tablespoon chopped chives
	pinch of chopped gingerroot
2	teaspoons crushed red pepper flakes

TUNA

4	(6-ounce) tuna steaks
1/4	cup black pepper
2	tablespoons canola oil
4	cups spinach

1/2	diced red bell pepper
10	chopped chives
1/4	cup prepared wasabi

METHOD

1. For the sauce, combine all ingredients in a bowl; mix well. Let stand at room temperature 30 minutes.

2. For the tuna, press both sides of the steaks into the pepper, coating well. Heat oil in a sauté pan till very hot. Add steaks; sear 10 seconds on each side. Remove to a board.

3. Add spinach to the pan and sauté just till wilted. Remove to 4 large plates. Slice tuna thinly across the grain and arrange in a star pattern over spinach.

4. Garnish with bell pepper, chives and wasabi. Top with sauce.

1/2 cup = 4 oz • 1 gal = 4 qts = 8 pts = 16 cups = 128 oz • 1 qt = 4 cups = 32 oz • 1 pt = 16 oz = 2 cups

EGGPLANT MEDALLIONS WITH JUMBO LUMP CRAB MEAT

INGREDIENTS ———————————————————————— Serves 4

HOLLANDAISE SAUCE

1	stick butter
2	egg yolks
1	tablespoon lemon juice
	dash of Tabasco sauce
1/4	cup white wine

MEUNIÈRE SAUCE

1/2	cup Veal Glace (page 134)
1/2	cup white wine
2	tablespoons lemon juice
1	stick butter, chopped

EGGPLANT AND CRAB MEAT MEDALLIONS

	canola oil for frying
1/2	cup milk
1/4	cup Original Chef's Grill Plus
1	peeled and sliced eggplant
2	cups corn flour
12	(3-inch) chive stems
1	recipe Sautéed Lump Crab Meat (page 99)

SAUCE DESIGN

2	tablespoons heavy cream
2	tablespoons sour cream

METHOD

1. For the Hollandaise Sauce, melt the butter in a saucepan over low heat. Cool to room temperature. Blend the egg yolks, lemon juice and Tabasco sauce in a metal bowl. Heat the wine in a small saucepan. Flambé and whisk gradually into the egg yolk mixture. Cook mixture over a double boiler, whisking continuously till firm peaks form. Remove from the heat; whisk in butter using a circular motion.

2. For the Meunière Sauce, combine the Veal Glace, wine and lemon juice in a saucepan; mix well. Cook till reduced by half. Remove from the heat and add the butter gradually, whisking till smooth after each addition. Keep warm.

3. For the medallions, preheat oil to 350 degrees in a deep fryer or electric skillet. Mix the milk and Chef's Grill Plus in a bowl. Dip the eggplant into the milk mixture and coat with corn flour. Fry till golden brown; drain on paper towels.

4. For the assembly, combine the Sauce Design ingredients in a bowl; mix well. Pour into a squeeze bottle. Spoon the Meuniére Sauce onto the plates and decorate with Sauce Design. Place the medallions on the center of the plates and top each with prepared Sautéed Lump Crab Meat. Drizzle with Hollandaise Sauce and garnish with chives.

3 tsp = 1 tbsp • 2 tbsp = 1/8 cup • 4 tbsp = 1/4 cup • 5 tbsp + 1 tsp = 1/3 cup • 1 cup = 8 oz

CAJUN FETTUCINI

1/4	cup butter	2	tablespoons tomato paste
1/4	pound julienned Andouille sausage	1/3	cup white wine
1/4	cup chopped green onions	1/4	cup lemon juice
1	tablespoon chopped garlic	3/4	cup grated Romano cheese
1	cup chopped mushrooms		salt to taste
1/4	pound (peeled) crawfish tail meat		white pepper to taste
1/4	pound baby shrimp	1/2	pound cooked fettucini
1	cup heavy cream		grated Romano cheese to taste

METHOD

1. Melt butter in a large sauté pan. Add the next 6 ingredients; sauté for 3 minutes. Blend the cream and tomato paste in a small bowl.

2. Add wine, lemon juice and cream mixture to the sauté pan; mix well. Cook for 3 minutes to reduce. Stir in 3/4 cup cheese and season with salt and pepper.

3. Add the pasta to the sauce; toss to coat well. Cook till the pasta is heated through. Serve with additional cheese. This popular recipe, along with Berries Denise on page 157, was requested by *Gourmet* magazine.

Always take a good look at what you're about to eat. It's not so important to know what it is, but it's critical to know what it was.
—Anonymous

1/2 cup = 4 oz • 1 gal = 4 qts = 8 pts = 16 cups = 128 oz • 1 qt = 4 cups = 32 oz • 1 pt = 16 oz = 2 cups

CORLEONE

1/2	cup sliced and blanched almonds		1/2	tablespoon cinnamon
1/4	cup pecans		1	teaspoon nutmeg
1/4	cup chopped white chocolate		6	scoops vanilla ice cream
1/4	cup chopped dark chocolate		1	cup honey
1/2	cup graham cracker crumbs			fresh mint leaves

METHOD

1. Combine first 7 ingredients in a food processor. Process till finely chopped. Transfer to a shallow dish.

2. Roll the scoops of ice cream in crumb mixture, coating evenly. Place in martini glasses and drizzle with honey. Garnish with mint.

Chocolate is a perfect food,
as wholesome as it is delicious,
a beneficent restorer of
exhausted power.
—Baron Justus von Liebig

3 tsp = 1 tbsp • 2 tbsp = 1/8 cup • 4 tbsp = 1/4 cup • 5 tbsp + 1 tsp = 1/3 cup • 1 cup = 8 oz

BERRIES DENISE

TULIP CUPS

1	egg	3/4	cup flour
2	egg whites	1/4	cup ground almonds
1/3	cup canola oil	2	teaspoons vanilla extract
1	cup sugar		

ASSEMBLY

1	recipe Sauce Design (page 154)	1	pint fresh blueberries
1	recipe Raspberry Coulis (page 144)		fresh mint leaves
4	(6-ounce) scoops favorite ice cream		
1	pint fresh raspberries		

METHOD

1. For the tulip cups, preheat oven to 350 degrees. Combine all ingredients in a mixing bowl; mix well. Ladle 1/4 cup of the mixture at a time onto the center of a greased cookie sheet to form a 7-inch circle. Bake till edge of cookie is brown. Remove immediately from cookie sheet with a metal spatula; mold around the bottom of a glass tumbler to form tulip shape. Repeat with remaining batter. Cool cups completely.

2. For the assembly, spoon the coulis onto dessert plates and drizzle with Sauce Design from a squeeze bottle. Drag a wooden pick through Sauce Design to create desired effect.

3. Scoop ice cream into tulip cups and top with remaining raspberries and blueberries. Place on dessert plates and garnish with mint leaves.

1/2 cup = 4 oz • 1 gal = 4 qts = 8 pts = 16 cups = 128 oz • 1 qt = 4 cups = 32 oz • 1 pt = 16 oz = 2 cups

DESSERTS

If your dinner makes a statement, surely the dessert is the exclamation point! The great thing about the recipes in this chapter is that most can be prepared in advance—then it takes only a few moments to assemble, garnish and serve.

While I was trained in the basics of baking, I didn't have the same opportunity to experiment and be as creative as I have with other cooking techniques. With most preparations, you can "massage" the recipe until it reaches the final stage. But you can't do that with desserts or with baking; it's too late in the final stage if you haven't followed the recipe as it was written. Baking is a science, and like a computer, what you put in, is what you get out. So you'll understand my hesitation when my sister asked me to create a new dessert a few years back.

Denise had just come back from Atlanta, raving about a dessert that she had indulged in at Capriccio's restaurant. She recalled everything about it: "The presentation was beautiful . . . it was sweet and light . . . and it was the perfect ending to my meal!" Now even though I had never seen the dessert or tasted it, she wanted me to create it "from scratch" and add it to the restaurant menu. I was a little intimidated, but with a lot of encouragement, I headed to the kitchen for a Command Performance. When I was finished with my re-creation, I presented the dish to Denise with a little flourish. She took a look, tasted it, and pronounced it, "Incredible!" After that, all the dessert needed was a name. It seemed only right to call it *Berries Denise*.

May I offer a word of advice? ***Always listen to your sister.*** *Berries Denise* has become one of the most-requested desserts on the menu at my restaurants. Thanks, Denise!

CHOCOLATE BROWNIES

3	sticks butter	1	tablespoon vanilla extract
2	tablespoons espresso grounds	12	small scoops vanilla ice cream
1 1/2	pounds broken dark chocolate	1	recipe Caramel Sauce (page 145)
6	eggs	1	recipe Chocolate Sauce (page 145)
3/4	cup flour	12	fanned strawberries
2 1/4	cups sugar		

METHOD

1. Preheat oven to 350 degrees. Spray a 9×12-inch baking dish with nonstick cooking spray. Combine butter, espresso grounds and chocolate in a double boiler. Heat till butter and chocolate melt, stirring to mix well.

2. Combine next 4 ingredients in a mixing bowl; mix well. Add chocolate mixture gradually, stirring constantly till smooth. Pour into prepared baking dish.

3. Bake at 350 degrees for 25 minutes. Cool on a wire rack. Cut into squares and place on microwave-safe plates. Microwave on high for one minute to reheat.

4. Top brownies with ice cream and drizzle with Caramel Sauce and Chocolate Sauce. Garnish with strawberries.

Chocolate is a perfect food.
—Baron Justus von Liebig

3 tsp = 1 tbsp • 2 tbsp = 1/8 cup • 4 tbsp = 1/4 cup • 5 tbsp + 1 tsp = 1/3 cup • 1 cup = 8 oz

DESSERT DRINKS—DOUBLE GODIVA, FROZEN GRASSHOPPER AND THE MITZI

DOUBLE GODIVA

3/4 ounce Godiva chocolate liqueur

3/4 ounce Godiva white chocolate liqueur

1/2 ounce Irish cream

1/2 ounce Stolichnaya vanilla vodka

1 1/2 cups vanilla ice cream

whipped cream

1 tablespoon shaved chocolate

FROZEN GRASSHOPPER

1 1/2 ounces green crème de menthe

1 ounce white crème de cacao

1 1/2 cups vanilla ice cream

whipped cream

THE MITZI

1 ounce Irish whiskey

3/4 ounce dark crème de cacao

3/4 ounce hazelnut liqueur

1 1/2 cups macadamia ice cream

whipped cream

METHOD

1. For the Double Godiva, combine the first 5 ingredients in a blender; blend till smooth. Pour into a poco grande glass. Garnish with whipped cream and chocolate.

2. For the Frozen Grasshopper, combine the first 3 ingredients in a blender; blend till smooth. Pour into a poco grande glass. Garnish with whipped cream.

3. For The Mitzi, combine the first 4 ingredients in a blender; blend till smooth. Pour into a poco grande glass. Garnish with whipped cream.

1/2 cup = 4 oz • 1 gal = 4 qts = 8 pts = 16 cups = 128 oz • 1 qt = 4 cups = 32 oz • 1 pt = 16 oz = 2 cups

BUMPER'S APPLE CRISP

1	tablespoon softened butter	2	beaten eggs
1	cup sugar	2	Granny Smith apples
3/4	cup flour	1/2	teaspoon cinnamon
1 1/2	teaspoons baking powder	6	scoops vanilla ice cream

METHOD

1. Preheat oven to 350 degrees. Spread butter in a 9-inch round baking dish. Combine next 4 ingredients in a mixing bowl; mix well. Let stand covered for 30 minutes.

2. Peel apples and cut into thin slices. Place in prepared baking dish. Drizzle with batter. Bake 35 minutes.

3. Spoon into serving dishes and sprinkle with cinnamon. Serve warm with ice cream.

Some things you have to do every day. Eating seven apples on Saturday night instead of one a day just isn't going to get the job done.
—*Jim Rohn*

3 tsp = 1 tbsp • 2 tbsp = 1/8 cup • 4 tbsp = 1/4 cup • 5 tbsp + 1 tsp = 1/3 cup • 1 cup = 8 oz

BANANA BREAD PUDDING

INGREDIENTS ———————————————————————— Serves 12

1	(3-foot) loaf stale French bread		1	cup heavy cream
1	cup packed light brown sugar		2	tablespoons vanilla extract
3/4	cup sugar		1	cup raisins
3	eggs		2	peeled, chopped bananas
2	cups half-and-half		1	stick butter, chopped

METHOD

1. Preheat the broiler. Slice the bread and arrange on a baking sheet. Broil just till toasted. Arrange in a 9×12-inch baking dish. Reduce the oven to 450 degrees.

2. Combine half the brown sugar and the next 5 ingredients in a large mixing bowl; mix well. Pour over toasted bread. Sprinkle with raisins and bananas; press gently.

3. Cover with foil; bake 20 minutes. Dot with butter and sprinkle with remaining 1/2 cup brown sugar. Bake uncovered for 5 minutes longer.

Other things are just food.
But chocolate's chocolate.
—Patrick Skene Catling

1/2 cup = 4 oz • 1 gal = 4 qts = 8 pts = 16 cups = 128 oz • 1 qt = 4 cups = 32 oz • 1 pt = 16 oz = 2 cups

SOUFFLÉS

1/4	cup melted butter	1 1/2	cups heavy cream
1 1/2	cups sugar	2	tablespoons butter
2	eggs	12	egg whites
1	egg yolk	2	cups vanilla ice cream
1/2	cup flour	1/4	cup Grand Marnier
1	tablespoon vanilla extract	1/4	cup powdered sugar

METHOD

1. Preheat oven to 375 degrees. Coat 6 oven safe 8-ounce ramekins with melted butter and dust with 1/2 cup sugar. Knock out the excess.

2. Combine remaining sugar and the next 4 ingredients in a mixing bowl; mix well. Heat cream in a heavy saucepan. Add egg mixture to cream very gradually, stirring constantly. Bring to a boil, stirring constantly. Remove from heat and mix in 2 tablespoons butter. Cool to room temperature.

3. Beat egg whites in a mixing bowl till stiff peaks form. Fold into cooled mixture. Spoon into prepared ramekins. Bake 20 minutes.

4. Melt ice cream in a saucepan over low heat. Stir in Grand Marnier; keep warm. Dust soufflés with powdered sugar and serve with prepared sauce.

Chemically speaking, chocolate really is the world's perfect food.
—Michael Levine

INDIVIDUAL VALRHONA CHOCOLATE CAKES

INGREDIENTS ———————— Serves 6

11   ounces Valrhona semisweet chocolate
11   ounces unsalted butter
6   eggs
6   egg yolks
1 1/4 cups flour
3/4   cup sugar
1 1/2 cups vanilla ice cream

METHOD

1. Preheat oven to 350 degrees. Spray six 8-ounce baking cups with nonstick cooking spray and dust with flour, shaking out the excess. Combine chocolate and butter in a double boiler. Heat over simmering water just till melted, stirring constantly to blend; remove from heat.

2. Combine the next 4 ingredients in a mixing bowl; mix well. Add chocolate and mix till smooth. Spoon equally into prepared cups.

3. Bake 7 minutes. Allow cups to cool slightly on a wire rack and invert onto serving plates. Serve with ice cream.

Cool the Individual Valrhona Chocolate Cakes completely and reheat in the microwave for one minute, if preferred. Also good served with English Toffee White Chocolate Ice Cream.

ENGLISH TOFFEE WHITE CHOCOLATE ICE CREAM

INGREDIENTS ———————— Serves 14

6   egg yolks
1   cup sour cream
1/2   cup white crème de cacao
2   cups sugar
5   Heath bars, crushed
1   cup chopped white chocolate
1   quart milk
1   quart heavy cream

METHOD

1. Combine the first 6 ingredients in a bowl; mix well. Combine with the milk and cream in a 6-quart ice cream freezer.

2. Follow the manufacturer's instructions. Serve immediately or store in freezer up to 2 weeks.

My tongue is smiling.
—Abigail Trillin, aged four, after eating chocolate ice-cream, quoted by her father, Calvin Trillin, in Alice, Let's Eat

CHOCOLATE PECAN TART

PIE SHELL

1	egg	3 1/4	cups flour
1	egg yolk	1/3	teaspoon salt
1/2	cup sugar	3	sticks butter, chopped

PIE

1	stick melted butter		pinch of salt
1	cup light corn syrup	1 1/4	cups chopped pecans
1	cup sugar	1	cup melted baking chocolate
3	large beaten eggs		vanilla ice cream
1	teaspoon vanilla extract	1	recipe Caramel Sauce (page 145)

METHOD

1. For the pie shell, combine first 5 ingredients in a mixing bowl. Add butter and mix by hand till butter is completely incorporated. Shape into a ball.

2. Roll dough into a circle on a lightly floured surface. Roll dough over a rolling pin and transfer to a 12-inch tart pan. Press into pan and trim the edge. Chill in refrigerator.

3. For the pie, preheat oven to 375 degrees. Combine first 6 ingredients in a bowl. Add pecans and chocolate; mix well. Pour into chilled pie shell.

4. Bake 25 minutes. Let stand on a wire rack 15 minutes before serving. Serve with ice cream and drizzle with Caramel Sauce.

There are four basic food groups: milk chocolate, dark chocolate, white chocolate, and chocolate truffles.
—Unknown

3 tsp = 1 tbsp • 2 tbsp = 1/8 cup • 4 tbsp = 1/4 cup • 5 tbsp + 1 tsp = 1/3 cup • 1 cup = 8 oz

EMERALD COAST KEY LIME PIE

GRAHAM CRACKER PIE SHELL

2	cups graham cracker crumbs	1/4	cup sugar
1/4	cup melted butter	1	egg white

PIE

6	egg yolks	3/4	cup lime juice
18	ounces sweetened condensed milk		whipped cream
1/2	cup sour cream		slices of lime or kiwifruit

METHOD

1. For the pie shell, preheat oven to 325 degrees. Combine all ingredients in a mixing bowl; mix well. Press over the bottom and sides of a 9-inch pie pan. Bake 8 to 10 minutes or till light brown. Cool to room temperature.

2. For the pie, reduce oven temperature to 275 degrees. Combine egg yolks with condensed milk and sour cream in a mixing bowl; mix well. Add lime juice; mix till smooth. Pour into pie shell.

3. Bake 15 to 20 minutes, turning pie after about 8 minutes to cook evenly. Cool on a wire rack. Chill in refrigerator. Garnish servings with whipped cream and a slice of lime or kiwifruit.

My advice to you is not to inquire why or whither, but just enjoy your ice cream while it's on your plate.
—Thornton Wilder

1/2 cup = 4 oz • 1 gal = 4 qts = 8 pts = 16 cups = 128 oz • 1 qt = 4 cups = 32 oz • 1 pt = 16 oz = 2 cups

SPECIAL EVENTS

It has been my great pleasure to serve quite a number of celebrities over the last 19 years. A lot of it was being in the right place at the right time. It also has to do with working hard, being open to new experiences, and doing everything I could to make my customers happy. At the restaurant, and whenever we cater, I say: "The answer is yes—what's the question?" That's been my motto. If we can do anything to make our customers' dining experience more enjoyable, we will.

Friends of mine have said, "Tim, you must be one of the luckiest guys on earth . . . cooking for Cybill Shepherd, Kathryn Crosby, and Timothy Hutton . . . creating a special dish for Tammy Cochran and escorting her to the 35th Annual Country Music Awards . . !" It's true; I have been blessed. But this is also true: the harder I worked, the more opportunities I had—some of them quite incredible.

A perfect example is when I was asked to become Chef de Cuisine for Amy Grant and Vince Gill's wedding reception. Amy and Vince were in Destin, had heard about the restaurant and came by for dinner. We visited briefly, and I knew they must have enjoyed my cuisine because they asked me to propose a menu for their wedding reception—which was in two weeks! Some time later, Amy showed up at one of my classes in Nashville. She surprised the class by serving as my assistant chef.

When I began my career as a chef, Chef Philippe, my mentor, taught me that preparing food was really about making people happy. Being a chef is something I can do to create joyful memories for others. It's something I can share with others. I am proud to say that I am a living example of the lessons I learned from an extraordinary teacher, Chef Parola: Make people happy—and keep it simple.

One evening I was fortunate enough to have music superstars Amy Grant and Vince Gill dine at my restaurant. Vince ordered the Pecan-Crusted Grouper served over Celery-Garlic Mashed Potatoes and topped with a Honey Worcestershire Sauce—a dish that's been on my menu for years. Both Amy and Vince said that they had enjoyed their meals immensely. After some casual conversation, I had the opportunity to arrange a golf tee-time for them the next morning. Not long after I received a phone call, asking me if I would consider catering their wedding reception in Nashville!

For the reception, I decided to create a special appetizer, Seared Tuna Rare Won Ton. This appetizer was passed among the 500-plus guests as they waited for the bride and groom to enter the wedding tent. And, speaking of tents, I cooked under a tent on Amy's driveway, using outdoor grills, bottled water, and several warming ovens. Take about a primitive kitchen—there was no kitchen! My assistants and I prepped two solid days prior to the event. We made Homemade Mozzarella by hand—in the back yard! On the day of the event, I was so busy that I never had a chance to look up until the very end when their publicist came over to "get more of the story."

continued on next page

AMY'S TUNA WON TONS

INGREDIENTS ———————————————————————————————— Serves 8

1/4	cup soy sauce		1	(8-ounce) sushi-grade Yellowfin tuna fillet
1/4	cup honey		1/2	cup black pepper
	pinch of chopped garlic		1	tablespoon canola oil
1	quart peanut oil		1	cup spinach
4	won ton wrappers		1	teaspoon finely chopped pickled ginger

METHOD

1. For the glaze, combine the soy sauce, honey and garlic in a saucepan; mix. Cook till reduced by half. Remove from heat and cool to room temperature.

2. For the won tons, preheat the peanut oil to 350 degrees. Cut the won ton wrappers into halves diagonally. Add to the heated oil and fry till brown and crisp; drain on paper towels.

3. For the tuna, press fillet into the pepper, coating both sides well. Heat the canola oil in a sauté pan and add the fillet. Sear briefly on both sides. Add the spinach and sauté just till wilted.

4. For the assembly, cut the tuna into thin slices. Place one slice on each won ton. Top with spinach and drizzle with soy glaze. Garnish with pickled ginger.

Two days after the wedding, a reporter from the TV show *"EXTRA"* came to my restaurant in Destin to interview me. *"EXTRA"* reported that Vince and Amy had been to my restaurant several weeks earlier, had dined on Chef Creehan's cuisine and that, "They *had* to have it." After all the media attention, people would come to the restaurant and say—without even looking at the menu— "I want what Amy and Vince had."

To save my staff a lot of confusion and explaining, we simply re-named the two dishes that couple had declared their favorites, "Amy's Tuna Won Tons" and "Grouper Vince." Both dishes consistently hit the "top of the charts" at my restaurant!

GROUPER VINCE

INGREDIENTS ———————————————————————— Serves 4

HONEY WORCESTERSHIRE SAUCE

1/2	cup honey	1	tablespoon (or more) cornstarch
1/4	cup Worcestershire sauce	1	tablespoon (or more) water
1/4	cup Veal Stock (page 134)		

GROUPER

1/4	cup Original Chef's Grill Plus	4	(6-ounce) grouper fillets
1/2	cup milk	1/4	cup canola oil
1/2	cup white flour	1	batch Celery-Garlic Mashed Potatoes (page 152)
1	cup J.W. Renfro's pecan flour	12	whole chives

METHOD

1. For the sauce, bring the honey, Worcestershire sauce and Veal Stock to a boil in a saucepan. Blend the cornstarch and water in a small bowl. Add to the Worcestershire sauce mixture and cook till thickened, stirring constantly. Keep warm.

2. For the grouper, preheat oven to 400 degrees. Blend the Chef's Grill Plus and milk in a dish. Mix the white flour and pecan flour in a shallow dish. Dip the fillets into the milk wash and coat with the flour mixture.

3. Heat the oil in a large ovenproof sauté pan. Add the fillets and sauté till brown on one side. Turn the fish and place in the oven; bake 10 minutes.

4. To serve, spoon the Celery-Garlic Mashed Potatoes onto the serving plates. Place the grouper on the potatoes and top with sauce. Garnish with whole or chopped chives.

In 1998 I was very excited to be going to Tokyo, Japan to participate in Foodex for the United States Department of Agriculture—an amazing food and beverage show that features products from around the globe. During the stay I cooked for 150 Japanese guests at the Cordon Bleu School and did three demonstrations each day at the American Pavilion. The highlight of the trip was a lunch I prepared for the United States Ambassador to Japan, former Speaker of the House Thomas Foley. We wanted to showcase United States agricultural products. This is one of the dishes he enjoyed for lunch that day.

PAN-SAUTÉED REDFISH WITH KEY LIME TOMATO SAUCE

INGREDIENTS ———————————————————————————————— Serves 6

KEY LIME TOMATO SAUCE

1/2	cup white wine		1/2	chopped tomato
1	cup heavy cream		1	tablespoon sugar
1/4	cup Key lime juice		1	stick softened butter
1	teaspoon chopped garlic			salt to taste
1	teaspoon chopped shallots			white pepper to taste

REDFISH

1/4	cup Original Chef's Grill Plus		2	cups white flour
1/2	cup milk		1/2	cup canola oil
6	(6-ounce) redfish fillets		1	tablespoon chopped chives

METHOD

1. For the sauce, combine the first 7 ingredients in a saucepan. Cook till reduced by half. Add butter gradually, stirring till melted after each addition. Season with salt and pepper. Keep warm.

2. For the fish, preheat oven to 450 degrees. Blend the Chef's Grill Plus and milk in a shallow dish. Dip the fillets into the milk mixture and coat with the flour.

3. Heat the oil in an ovenproof sauté pan. Add fillets and sauté till brown on the bottom. Turn the fillets and place in the oven. Bake 10 minutes. Place on serving plates and top with sauce. Garnish with chives.

In the summer of 1999 I was selected by *Cooking Light®* magazine to participate in their Shining Stars GrandStand Event held at Turner Field in Atlanta, Georgia. I was one of five chefs selected from across the nation to prepare a heart-healthy dish that was representative of my culinary style. I chose a dish that's been popular at my restaurants for years, Thai Chicken Salad. This dish proves that many flavors are available to us that have nothing to do with high-fat ingredients.

THAI CHICKEN SALAD

INGREDIENTS
Serves 6

1 tablespoon vegetable oil	1/4 teaspoon chile paste
1 cup quartered mushrooms	1 minced garlic clove
1/2 cup rice vinegar	4 cups chopped chicken breasts (about 4)
1/2 cup reduced-sodium soy sauce	4 cups thinly sliced Napa (Chinese) cabbage
1/4 cup pineapple juice	1/2 cup thinly sliced red cabbage
1 tablespoon chopped fresh mint	4 cups thinly sliced romaine lettuce leaves
1 teaspoon minced gingerroot	1 cup yellow or red bell pepper strips
1 teaspoon fish sauce	1/2 cup alfalfa sprouts
1 teaspoon dark sesame oil	

METHOD

1. Heat the vegetable oil in a nonstick skillet over medium-high heat. Add mushrooms and sauté 3 minutes. Combine the mushrooms with the next 9 ingredients in a bowl. Add the chicken and toss to coat well. Marinate in the refrigerator for 30 minutes.

2. Combine the Napa cabbage, red cabbage and romaine in a bowl and mix well. Spoon onto 6 serving plates. Top with chicken mixture. Sprinkle with the bell pepper strips and alfalfa sprouts.

Poultry is for the cook what canvas is to the painter.
—Brillat-Savarin

In the blockbuster movie "Titanic," di Caprio's Jack Dawson asks Winslet's Rose DeWitt Bukater, "Wanna go to a *real* party?" My staff and I wanted to have a *real* party for New Year's Eve, 1998. My restaurant was new; we needed something spectacular to bring in the New Year. I decided to re-create the last dinner served on the Titanic in the luxury liner's first-class dining room. We hired professional actors to play the Unsinkable Molly Brown, Lucille Polk Cart, and Mr. and Mrs. John Jacob Astor, to name a few of the ship's influential passenger list. We wanted to be as authentic as possible, starting with the table settings and the invitations, which we had engraved with the logo design from the White Star Line. We even had a candy dish made by a company that acquired design rights from the original manufascturer of the Titanic's china service. Each couple left that night with a commemorative candy dish as a gift. The evening was truly magical! The recipe that follows was the third course in that dinner—and my favorite re-creation.

POACHED SALMON MOUSSELINE WITH A TARRAGON CREAM SAUCE

INGREDIENTS ———————————————————————————— Serves 6

MOUSSELINE

1	pound salmon	2	teaspoons lemon juice
3	large eggs	1	tablespoon salt
2	cups heavy cream	1	teaspoon white pepper
1	tablespoon dry sherry		

TARRAGON CREAM SAUCE

2	cups heavy cream	2	tablespoons chopped fresh tarragon
3	tablespoons tarragon vinegar		salt to taste
1/2	cup tomato paste		white pepper to taste
2	tablespoons lemon juice		

METHOD

1. For the Mousseline, preheat oven to 350 degrees. Process the salmon in a food processor till puréed. Add eggs and mix well. Add the next 5 ingredients gradually, processing constantly till smooth. Spoon the mixture into 4 to 6-ounce buttered baking ramekins. Place ramekins in a baking pan with enough water to reach halfway up the sides of the ramekins. Bake 25 minutes. Let stand while preparing the cream sauce.

2. For the Tarragon Cream Sauce, combine all 7 ingredients in a saucepan and mix well. Bring to a boil, stirring constantly.

3. To serve, spoon some of the cream sauce onto the serving plates. Unmold the Mousseline onto the plates and top with additional cream sauce.

Miss Denise Creehan

Table No. 52

Seating Time: 8:30 p.m.

Eve 1998

Mr. and Mrs. John T. Creehan

Table No. 39

Seating Time: 7:30 p.m.

Titanic New Year's Eve 1998

WHITE STAR LINE
STATE ROOM
D
STATE ROOM

First - Class Menu

April 14, 1912

FIRST COURSE
Canapés à l' Amiral
Oysters à la Russe
Louis Jadot Pouilly-Fuissé

SECOND COURSE
Consommé Olga
Swanson Roato Sangiovese

THIRD COURSE
Poached Salmon Mousseline Tarragon Cream Sauce
Pichot Vouvray

FOURTH COURSE
Filet Mignon Lili
Perrin Gigondas

FIFTH COURSE
Sorbet Trio

SIXTH COURSE
Port Wine Glazed Duckling with Applesauce
Roasted Stuffed Quail on Braised Escarole
Mongeard-Mogneret Savigny le Beaune

SEVENTH COURSE
Asparagus Salad with Saffron Vinaigrette

EIGHTH COURSE
Assorted Cheeses and Patés

NINTH COURSE
Chocolate Painted Eclairs with Chocolate Truffles
Schramsberg Blanc de Noir

When *Country Weekly* contacted me about doing a "chef-artist segment" in their magazine, I had no idea that I was going to be a part of something so awesome. The magazine told me I could choose any dish I wanted, to cook with Tammy Cochran, a rising star on the Country Music scene. My initial thought was to prepare one of my signature dishes to make the photo shoot less stressful. Then a video arrived featuring Tammy's Top Ten song, "Angels in Waiting," which told the story of her two brothers who died of cystic fibrosis. "Angels in Waiting" became the inspiration for an original dish—a dish created to pay tribute to Tammy and to her brothers. Tammy's Fish Trio was a weave of salmon and Mahi-Mahi that represented the brother's bond, and tuna, cut on the bias and standing, represented Tammy's growing career and her future success. Angel hair pasta tied in to the title track. And the fried green tomatoes were pure *Country Weekly*.

Tammy was a pleasure to work with. And, much to my surprise, she invited me to escort her to the 2001 Country Music Awards, a memory I will always treasure.

TAMMY'S FISH TRIO

INGREDIENTS ———————————————————————— Serves 6

SMOKED TOMATO SAUCE

I	peeled cored tomato
1/4	yellow onion
I	cup Chicken Stock (page 130)
1/2	cup heavy cream

2	tablespoons tomato paste
1/4	chipotle pepper in adobo sauce
	salt to taste

MUSHROOM SAUCE

2	cups heavy cream
1/2	cup chopped Portabello mushrooms
1/4	cup chopped green onions

I	teaspoon chopped garlic
1/2	cup grated Romano cheese
	freshly ground black pepper to taste

METHOD

1. For the Smoked Tomato Sauce, prepare a smoker. Smoke the tomato and onion over low heat for 30 minutes. Combine with the next 5 ingredients in a food processor; process till smooth. Spoon into a saucepan and cook over medium heat till reduced to a thick sauce consistency. Keep warm.

2. For the Mushroom Sauce, bring cream to a boil in a large sauté pan. Add the next 4 ingredients; mix well. Season with pepper. Cook till reduced by 1/3. Keep warm.

continued on next page

SALMON AND MAHI-MAHI WEAVE

1 (1 1/2 pound) boneless salmon fillet
1 (1 1/2 pound) boneless Mahi-Mahi fillet
2 quarts lightly salted water

FRIED GREEN TOMATOES

2 green tomatoes
   canola oil for frying
1/4 cup Original Chef's Grill Plus
1/2 cup milk
2 cups cornmeal

TUNA

1 (1-inch) Yellowfin tuna steak
1 tablespoon Herbs and Garlic Chef's
   Grill Plus

ASSEMBLY

1/2 pound cooked angel hair pasta
18 chives
2 peeled and thinly sliced lemons
1/2 cup chopped green onions

METHOD

1. For the weave, preheat oven to warm. Cut the fillets across the grain into slices 1/8 inch thick and at least 4 inches long. Weave 4 slices of each fish together to form a basket weave. Bring salted water to a low boil and carefully add the fish. Poach 3 to 5 minutes or till cooked through. Drain well and place in a baking dish. Keep warm in the low oven.

2. For the tuna, preheat a grill surface. Brush one side of the steak with half the Chef's Grill Plus. Place seasoned side down and grill till marked. Brush the top with the remaining Chef's Grill Plus and turn the steak. Grill to desired doneness. Cut into 6 triangles and keep warm.

3. For the tomatoes, cut into eight wedges. Preheat oil in a fryer or sauté pan. Mix the Chef's Grill Plus with the milk in a shallow dish. Dip the tomato wedges into the milk mixture and coat with the cornmeal. Fry in the heated oil till golden brown on both sides.

4. For the assembly, spoon the tomato sauce onto one side of each serving plate. Arrange 3 fried tomato wedges in the sauce on each plate. Toss pasta with the mushroom sauce to coat well. Roll into 6 cylinders with a two-pronged fork and place on side opposite tomatoes. Garnish with chives. Overlap the woven fish partially on the pasta facing the tomatoes. Top each with 3 slices of lemon. Stand the tuna next to the woven fish and garnish with onions.

My song, "Angels in Waiting," has inspired a lot of people. I didn't know it could inspire food. That's so cool.
—Tammy Cochran, Country Recording Artist

When Cajun food began to be nationally recognized in mid-80's, I was hired to do two events in one year that featured Cajun cuisine. The first was a Central Park bash given by Christine Jones, an actress who played Asa Buchanan's wife on "One Life to Live." The second event was held at the Bermuda Run Country Club in North Carolina, the Annual Crosby Open Golf Tournament. During the tournament, Kathryn Crosby presented a life-sized painting of Bing Crosby to the Country Club. That summer hundreds of people enjoyed Etouffé, my favorite Creole specialty! Celebrities at the golf tournament—to name a few—included Jimmy Dean, Roman Gabriel, Bruce Weitz of "Hill Street Blues," MacLean Stevenson, Alan Thicke, Leslie Nielsen, Tony Danza, and Tony Dow, who played Wally Cleaver in "Leave It to Beaver."

CRAWFISH ETOUFFÉ

INGREDIENTS ———————————————————————————————— Serves 6 to 8

2	sticks butter		3	cups tomato sauce
1	large chopped yellow onion		2	cups water
2	chopped celery ribs			salt to taste
1	chopped green bell pepper			black pepper to taste
1	tablespoon chopped garlic			cayenne pepper to taste
1	cup white flour		1	bunch green onions, chopped
2	pounds fresh crawfish tail meat		12	cups steamed rice

METHOD

1. Heat butter in a heavy saucepan and add the next 4 ingredients. Sauté 5 minutes. Stir in the flour gradually till all is incorporated.

2. Add the crawfish, tomato sauce and water and bring to a boil. Reduce heat and simmer for 30 minutes. Season with salt, black pepper and cayenne pepper.

3. Add additional water if needed to adjust the thickness. Add green onions. Serve over the steamed rice.

In China we have only three religions, but we have a hundred dishes we can make from rice.
—Chinese Proverb

In the winter of 1984 I was invited to the Hong Kong Hilton to cook for the American Harvest Promotion in their premier dining room. I was just 18 years old. I created and served dozens of French- and Louisiana-style dishes over a two-week period. The event was a huge success. I treasure the talented local chefs I worked with. I was honored to bring one of America's native cuisines to China. Oyster and Roasted Corn Soup was a favorite of both the locals and the tourists from around the world who dined with us. I was featured on "Good Morning, Hong Kong" and also in *China Daily News*.

OYSTER AND ROASTED CORN SOUP

INGREDIENTS ————————————————————————— Serves 8 to 10

4	cups fresh oysters		2	cups diced potatoes
2	tablespoons butter		1	teaspoon ground oregano
2	cups diced yellow onions			kernels cut from 4 ears of fresh corn
2	tablespoons chopped garlic		2	jalapenos fresh diced
3	chopped leeks (white part only)		3	cups heavy cream
1/2	cup flour			salt to taste
4	cups clam juice			

METHOD

1. Strain the oysters and reserve the liquid. Melt butter in a soup pot and add the onions, garlic and leeks. Sauté 5 minutes. Stir in the flour till bubbly.

2. Add the reserved liquid and the next 3 ingredients. Boil 15 minutes.

3. Toast the corn in a dry sauté pan till light brown. Add to the soup. Add the jalapenos, cream and oysters. Season with salt. Bring to a boil and reduce heat. Simmer 15 minutes.

I ate the oysters with their strong taste of the sea and their faint metallic taste that the cold white wine washed away, leaving only the sea taste and the succulent texture. . .
—*Ernest Hemingway,* A Moveable Feast

Cybill Shepherd and Don Johnson were filming "The Long Hot Summer," a movie for television, when I was working at Chef John Folse's restaurant in Donaldsonville, Louisiana. I was either 19 or 20 years old. Shepherd and Johnson had dined several times at the restaurant and they "took a liking" to what I called my classical spin on traditional Cajun and Creole cuisine. On Cybill's last night in town, she asked if I would ever consider coming to Malibu, California to prepare a private dinner for her and a few friends at her beach house. Would I? Six months later I was in Malibu, cooking a nine-course meal for "Cybill and Friends," mostly cast and crew of "Moonlighting." Among the guests were Paul LeMat of "American Graffiti," and a fresh young actor named Bruce Willis. Willis arrived fashionably late. In Hollywood that can be quite a wait . . . but everything went off without a hitch, and I scored with the Bananas Foster Cheesecake. Everyone loved it!

BANANAS FOSTER CHEESECAKE

INGREDIENTS ———————————————————————————— Serves 12

CRUST

3/4   cup graham cracker crumbs
1/4   cup sugar
1/3   cup melted butter

FILLING

2   pounds softened cream cheese
6   eggs
1   cup melted unsalted butter
2   cups sugar

2   tablespoons white crème de cacao
       banana liqueur to taste
2   tablespoons vanilla extract

SAUCE

1/2   cup unsalted butter
2   cups packed brown sugar
1   teaspoon cinnamon

7   thickly sliced bananas
1/3   cup banana liqueur
2/3   cup rum

METHOD

1.   For the crust, preheat oven to 325 degrees.

2.   Combine graham cracker crumbs, sugar and butter in a mixing bowl; mix well. Press over the bottom of a 10-inch springform pan.

3.   Bake till the edge is brown. Remove from the oven and cool.

4. For the filling, combine all ingredients inside a mixing bowl with a whip attachment. Mix at medium speed till smooth.

5. Pour into the prepared springform pan. Bake for 20 minutes. Reduce oven temperature to 250 degrees. Bake 30 minutes longer or till the center is firm to touch.

6. Turn off the oven. Allow cheesecake to cool in the closed oven for 20 minutes. Chill in the refrigerator for 4 hours. Cut into 12 wedges and place on serving plates.

7. For the sauce, combine butter, brown sugar and cinnamon in a sauté pan. Heat till butter and brown sugar melt, stirring to mix well. Add bananas, banana liqueur and rum. Flambé and cook till the bananas are tender. Spoon over sliced cheesecake and serve immediately.

Food should be prepared with butter and love.
—Swedish proverb

ALSO BY CHEF CREEHAN

Chef Tim Creehan's
Flavors of the Gulf Coast cookbook
ISBN 0-9634545-1-X

Packed with eye-popping pictures and incredible recipes culled from Chef Tim Creehan's years of experience as a restaurateur, *Flavors of the Gulf Coast* is a must-have in any collection. Online ordering available at timcreehan.com/cookbooks.

Chef Tim Creehan's Grill Plus® is a patented instant marinade and cooking sauce suitable for seasoning all types of food. There's virtually nothing it can't do in the kitchen, whether used as an instant marinade for seasoning, a base for milk wash, a zesty dip, or the heart of a sauce, Grill Plus® works magic on any food it touches. Online ordering available at chefsgrillplus.com.

Tim Creehan's
CUVEE 30A

As seen on *Emeril's Florida*, Cuvee 30A brings celebrity Chef Tim Creehan's award-winning signature dishes to South Walton's gorgeous 30Avenue.
Phone: 850-909-0111
Located at 30Avenue
12805 U.S. Highway 98, Suite D101
Inlet Beach, FL 32461
cuvee30a.com

INDEX